RANGE ROVER
SECOND GENERATION
THE COMPLETE STORY

RANGE ROVER
SECOND GENERATION
THE COMPLETE STORY

James Taylor

THE CROWOOD PRESS

First published in 2018 by
The Crowood Press Ltd
Ramsbury, Marlborough
Wiltshire SN8 2HR

www.crowood.com

British Library Cataloguing-in-Publication Data
A catalogue record for this book is available from the British Library.

ISBN 978 1 78500 473 5

Typeset by Jean Cussons Typesetting, Diss, Norfolk

Printed and bound in India by Parksons Graphics

CONTENTS

INTRODUCTION AND ACKNOWLEDGEMENTS

When I wrote my first book about the 38A Range Rover back in 2004, I was deeply conscious of the fact that there were many areas of the model's history that still needed to be researched. I'm pleased to say that I have been able to fill in many of the gaps in the story over the intervening fourteen years, and this book contains an account that is not only more in depth, but is also in some areas more accurate.

Even so, the business of researching the story behind the 38A Range Rover is probably far from finished. In preparing this latest book, I was astonished to discover how difficult it can be to unearth details of such things as the overseas special editions, and I don't doubt that there is more to say on some other aspects of the story as well. So if any readers are able to provide extra information, I'll be very pleased to hear from them through the publishers.

Meanwhile, I have to acknowledge that a vast number of people have contributed to the knowledge that this book contains. Over the years I have been able to talk to many Land Rover people who were involved with the 38A, and in particular to Malcolm Ainsley, Bill Baker, John Bilton, Roger Crathorne, Mike Gould, John Hall, Charlie Hughes, Mike Sampson, Graham Silvers, David Sneath and George Thomson. Some of these names, sadly, are no longer with us. I visited the assembly lines many times, drove multiple examples both on and off the road when they were new, and even managed to get myself invited to BMW's engine factory at Steyr in Austria to see the diesel engines being built.

Other information has come from a multitude of owners, enthusiasts, aftermarket specialists, and those who simply sold or fixed the vehicles. They know who they are, and they know I'm grateful. Finally, special thanks go to my long-time friend photographer Nick Dimbleby, who willingly and enthusiastically provided a lot of the pictures I've used in this book.

James Taylor
Oxfordshire
January 2018

TIMELINE

1994, September   Global announcement of new '38A' Range Rover.

1995, September   Automatic diesel models introduced.

1996, October   Autobiography custom-building scheme announced.

1998, September   Revised 'Thor' V8 engines.

1999, October   New fourth (Vogue) level of trim announced.
Facelift with masked headlamps and smoked indicator lenses.

2000, July   Land Rover Ltd sold to Ford Motor Company.

2002, February   Last 38A Range Rover built.

The distinctive promotional motif used when the second-generation Range Rover was introduced in 1994. The line of trees stretching into the distance was intended to suggest the infinite possibilities that ownership could bring.

CHAPTER ONE

DESIGN AND DEVELOPMENT

By the time Land Rover introduced the second-generation Range Rover in autumn 1994, the original model had been in production for no fewer than twenty-four years. Even then, its production life was not over, because Land Rover kept on making it for another eighteen months or so to ease the acceptance of the new model. The old one had developed such a following that the company was understandably nervous about how well the new one would go down.

Quite obviously, the first-generation Range Rover was an enormously hard act to follow. As its creator, Spen King, said to the author in the mid-1990s, it is one thing to design a completely new model that becomes impressive over the years, but a much harder task to follow that up with a replacement that has to be impressive from the start. So it is important not to underestimate the size of the task that was facing Land Rover in the mid-1980s when it began to contemplate how to replace the Range Rover. By global standards, it was still a small company – tiny when compared to Toyota, then, as now, the world's largest maker of four-wheel-drive vehicles – and by any standards replacing an icon like the Range Rover was a very tall order.

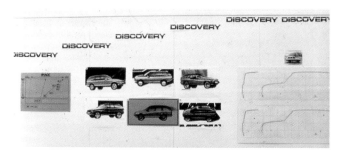

From 1988, the new Range Rover project became known as the Discovery programme. This picture of a wall in the styling studio shows some of the ideas that were then in play.

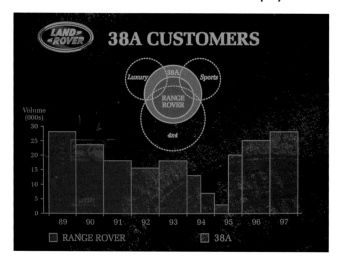

After the Discovery name was taken for the new vehicle that had been developed as Project Jay, the Range Rover project was renamed Pegasus. This slide was made for a presentation at the time.

When the Pegasus name began to attract unwelcome attention, John Hall changed the project name to 38A. This is a slide from another internal presentation.

It was not until 1988 that Land Rover really began to focus on creating a new Range Rover, and the design and engineering programme went through three stages between then and the vehicle's 1994 launch: first it was called Project Discovery, then it became Project Pegasus, and finally it became Project 38A. The six years of its development present a complicated story, which is more easily understood when divided into segments. So this chapter begins with the background to each of those three project stages, and then goes on to tell the detailed story of how each element of the vehicle came into being. But as a prelude to that, it is worth taking a look at what had happened before 1988.

FIRST THOUGHTS

A few ideas for a new Range Rover had been considered after Land Rover Ltd had become a standalone business within British Leyland in 1978. However, discussion on the subject was entirely theoretical, because nobody had identified a date by which such a new model might be needed, nor had anybody given any serious thought to what might be expected of that new model. There would, inevitably, be a new Range Rover one day. But for the time being, the old one was selling very well, thank you, and there were plans to make it a more luxurious vehicle than it had been when new in 1970. There was no real vision beyond that.

The earliest indication that Land Rover had started to take the challenge of a new Range Rover seriously dates from 1981. Land Rover's long-serving Chief Engineer, Tom Barton, retired that year, and his deputy Mike Broadhead took over from him. Broadhead initiated a concept study

within the Engineering Department that was known as Adventurer. Its aim was to investigate a rationalized range of Land Rovers and Range Rovers that would share as many common features as possible. These features would not be confined to such things as engines and gearboxes, but might also include a common body-chassis structure. This aspect of the study was handed to Gordon Bashford, a key figure in the design of the original Range Rover, who also retired that year and found himself immediately retained as a consultant on Adventurer.

In the Adventurer study, a great deal of effort was put into better packaging that would give more interior space for a given vehicle size. Gordon Bashford's part of it proposed some quite original ideas, but there was never any real chance that Adventurer would be anything other than a paper study. Land Rover were already too far down the road with a new Land Rover utility – introduced as the One Ten in 1983 – and were not going to need another all-new model for some years. However, Adventurer was not entirely forgotten. The concept of a rationalized range remained alive and well by 1985 – after Mike Broadhead had left and Bill Morris had become Chief Engineer – when it was revived as the twin Inca and Ibex projects.

THE INCA AND IBEX PROJECTS

By 1985 Land Rover was beginning to re-establish itself after a very difficult period in the early 1980s. The company's traditional overseas markets, notably in Africa, had collapsed under the twin impacts of government changes in overseas funding, and cheap, light 4×4 utilities made in

It could have happened: there were early discussions about making the new Range Rover a sort of people carrier, and this rendering from the Styling Department reflected that. The date appears to be early 1985, and the designer was George Thomson, who later took the lead on the second-generation Range Rover.

One of the full-size renderings for Range Rover during the Ibex phase is seen during a viewing at Drayton Road.

Japan. The company's core product, represented by the last of the Series III Land Rovers and the first of the One Ten and Ninety coil-sprung models, was struggling for overseas sales. In 1983 Land Rover had recorded its first ever annual loss, and new Managing Director Tony Gilroy was faced with the job of turning the company around.

His decision was to re-orient Land Rover towards developed countries, to make up losses in Africa by gains in Europe and the USA, and to do that he needed a product that would have the right appeal. The utility Land Rover, even in its latest coil-sprung One Ten and Ninety form, was not it, and the only solution was to make the Range Rover into a luxury-class product. So by 1985 there was a new regular production flagship variant called the Range Rover Vogue in showrooms, plans for introducing the Range Rover to the USA were being implemented, and a programme of future upgrades had been mapped out to make the Range Rover a more credible alternative to expensive luxury saloons.

In that climate, it is no surprise that somebody decided it would be wise to take a more serious look at the longer-term future of the Range Rover. So it was that the first proper thinking about a new Range Rover went into a pair of related projects that were known as Inca and Ibex. Land Rover was far from cash-rich at the time, and so the plan was to develop both utility Land Rovers and a new Range Rover from the same basic structure. There has been some confusion about which code name referred to which vehicle, but the discovery of some photographs of new Range Rover

proposals in a drawer in the old Styling Department (now known as Design) a few years ago makes clear that the Range Rover was Ibex.

Quite a lot of planning was done around these twin concepts, but neither progressed beyond the drawing board. Those who were involved remember that the Range Rover was to have an all-welded body, while the Land Rover would need a bolt-together construction to allow for overseas assembly and a large number of different variants. This fundamental divergence tended to drive the two designs in different directions, and in the end the designers decided it was not possible to build the two vehicles off a single common platform.

CHANGES OF OWNERSHIP (I)

Land Rover Ltd had been formed in 1978 as a standalone business under British Leyland, although of course the Land Rover marque had started life in 1948 as an offshoot of the old independent Rover Company. After a major reorganization in 1986, what had once been British Leyland became the Rover Group, and Land Rover Ltd retained its independence within that new group. However, British Leyland had been under government control since 1974, and by the end of the 1980s the Conservative government of Margaret Thatcher was pursuing a policy of privatization. So the Rover Group had to go, and the selected new owner was British Aerospace, who took nominal control in 1988.

One of the first things to happen under the new ownership was that the Rover Cars and Land Rover design and engineering departments were amalgamated. This was not universally liked – Spen King (by then retired) was among those who described it as a political move to prevent the two halves of the company from being sold separately if and when British Aerospace in turn decided to sell the Rover Group. Nevertheless, the amalgamation was beneficial to the development of the second-generation Range Rover, because the car specialists (who were needed to add the appropriate luxury touches) could more easily be seconded to the team who were developing it.

While work was being done on Inca and Ibex, Land Rover's business priorities were changing. Tony Gilroy had commissioned a market study to determine the best way for Land Rover to go forward, and during 1986 this made clear that there were important developments in the 4×4 market. On the one hand, the success of the Range Rover had led to the creation of a number of cheaper imitators, mostly made in Japan, that were aimed at family buyers and were selling strongly. On the other hand, there was a growing interest in the use of 4×4 vehicles to support outdoor sporting activities, and customers expected those vehicles to be as comfortable and easy to drive as a conventional car.

It was obvious that if Land Rover could develop a model that would cater for both of those market sectors, it could have a strong-selling product that would accelerate its return to long-term sustainability as a company. So by mid-1986, the number one product development priority at Land Rover had become Project Jay, which would be launched in 1989 as the Land Rover Discovery. One result was that Inca and Ibex simply withered on the vine. However, it is interesting that Project Jay reflected similar thinking: just as Inca and Ibex would have minimized costs by sharing major components, so the Jay vehicle minimized costs (and development time) by sharing its chassis and much of its drivetrain with the existing Range Rover.

SERIOUS DEVELOPMENTS

Project Discovery, 1988

The bulk of the design and engineering work on Project Jay was expected to be completed by the end of 1988, and this would allow Land Rover to start thinking about other new products again. But it was already obvious that some preliminary work could be done on the projected new Range Rover before the main design and engineering resources were freed up.

As a first step, Product Director Steve Schlemmer brought in John Hall from the Freight Rover light commercial vehicles side of the Rover Group, and appointed him as Group Chief Engineer. Hall's responsibility was for the Styling Department (as Design was then called) and Forward Engineering, and under the latter of course came planning for the new Range Rover. This was given the formal name of Project Discovery, and was run by a small team working under Bob Allsopp. Hall himself meanwhile spent most of

the year reviewing the scope of the project and how the business could cope with it.

From the start, Hall had to deal with certain fundamentals. At the time, Land Rover was committed to using permanent four-wheel-drive on all its vehicles. All Land Rover products were expected to have class-leading off-road abilities, and that meant the new Range Rover would need a two-range transfer gearbox. It would also have to give a cossetting on-road ride if it was to be a credible luxury car, and so independent suspension would have to be investigated as an alternative to Land Rover's traditional 'live' axles front and rear. Engines would need enough power to give good on-road performance, and enough torque to give excellent towing performance as well as the low-down grunt needed for off-road work.

As for size, the new model would need more passenger space than the existing Range Rover, where the 100in (2,540mm) wheelbase gave poor rear-seat legroom. So John Hall's team examined a range of wheelbase sizes between 106in (2,690mm) and 110in (2,795mm), finally settling on a size of 108in – or more precisely 2,745mm, because Land Rover was actually working to metric dimensions despite its continued traditional use of imperial measurements in model names. Two of those inches were to be inserted between the front axle and the front bulkhead, creating larger footwells for the front seat passengers and improving the vehicle's crash performance as well. The other 6in (150mm) were to be used mainly to increase legroom for rear-seat passengers, with a little extra for the boot area as well.

So this was going to be a large vehicle – far too large to have the monocoque construction that was universal in the luxury car market where Land Rover hoped it would succeed. Instead, it would need a traditional Land Rover ladder-frame chassis with a separate bodyshell mounted on top of it, although that bodyshell could be more modern in structure than the one on the existing Range Rover.

Project Pegasus, 1988–1990

At the end of 1988, the amalgamation of the Rover and Land Rover engineering teams began, and for a large part of 1989 the new Range Rover programme was more or less on hold while the Rover Group sorted itself out. Projected costs had already started to escalate alarmingly, and so this pause allowed the designers and engineers some time to think about how best to proceed.

It was in this fallow period that the project for the new Range Rover took on yet another new name. The project itself did not change: it was simply that Discovery had been chosen as the name for the Project Jay family 4×4 in the first few months of 1989. So the Range Rover, known up to that point as Project Discovery, now became Project Pegasus. It continued to tick over with Bob Allsopp in charge until Rover Group Chief Executive John Towers formally appointed John Hall as Project Director and authorized him to assemble a dedicated team to develop a new Range Rover. According to Hall, this was probably in late 1989, or possibly early 1990.

So the Project Pegasus team came together. John Hall appointed Mike Pendry as Chief Engineer. Working to him were Bob Allsopp as Chief Engineer, Vehicle Development, and Frank Bolderstone as Chief Engineer, Vehicle Layout. There were then eight 'component' teams, each under a team leader who reported to Mike Pendry. These teams covered chassis, body-in-white, body hardware, lower trim, upper trim, electrical (two teams) and powertrain systems (with sub-teams for engine, transmission and engine management systems).

In the beginning, only small numbers of engineers and designers were involved with Project Pegasus, and John Hall remembered that he had a china model of Pegasus, the winged horse, in his office. He found it a very useful tool for focusing the attention of the team on what the new Range Rover was all about. However, the small team gradually grew larger and larger, and at its peak the Pegasus team would consist of between 250 and 300 people (the number varies according to who is telling the story). For Land Rover, this was a far larger team than had ever been assembled before, although by motor industry standards it was a small team to deliver a product of such great ambition and importance as the new Range Rover.

Project 38A, 1990–1994

For the first couple of years, Land Rover was successful in keeping secret most of the work it was doing towards a new Range Rover. However, customer clinics, in which groups of potential buyers were shown pictures or mock-ups of the new vehicle without being told what it was, had begun to raise the project's public profile. The name of Pegasus had also leaked out to the media. Nobody is sure how, but there was a briefing for component suppliers in July 1990

and shortly after that, the first hints were made to UK police forces about the new vehicle. As John Hall remembered:

Pegasus was really a great name for motivating the team and, you know, getting excitement, but unfortunately… people outside the business – either through talking to people within Rover or talking to our supplier base – also found it a very interesting and exciting name, and we started getting a lot of pressure from journalists. So we decided to change the name of the project to the name of the building that we worked at up at Solihull.

In fact the Pegasus team was based in two adjoining buildings, Building 38A being their studio and design headquarters, while Building 38 next door was the workshop. From mid-1990, the new Range Rover became Project 38A, and, continued John Hall, 'that was tremendous because, you know, "Project 38A" sort of goes … whoof, very boring!'

Project 38A then remained the codename for the new Range Rover right through until production began in 1994, and was never formally changed. However, in later years many people at Land Rover began to call the model a P38A, and later still this became corrupted to P38. Interestingly, UK police forces would always refer to the second-generation Range Rover as Pegasus, the name by which it was introduced to them in 1990.

THE KEY ELEMENTS

Chassis

Once the new model's wheelbase size had been established as 108in (2,745mm), design was able to progress. Chassis engineering was entrusted to a team led by John Kellett, and unsurprisingly, the chassis frame took shape as a traditional ladder-frame type with box-section side members. Some cross-members were also of box-section construction, but others were tubular, and wherever possible, the designers did what they could to save weight while maintaining robustness. Along their length, the side members had graduated thickness, and therefore stiffness, to provide good crash deformation characteristics. In plan view, they also tapered in much more at the front than on any other existing Land Rover chassis.

Overall, the new chassis finished up stiffer than that of

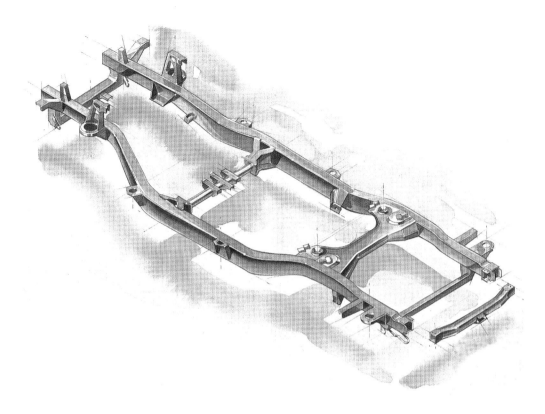

The new chassis frame, viewed here from the back, was quite different from that of the existing Range Rover, with much more curvature of the side members in plan view.

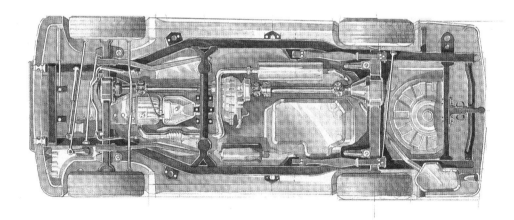

Packaging of the mechanical components was carefully arranged to give them maximum protection in off-road use and against collision damage.

the first-generation Range Rover, with thicker metal everywhere. This did put plenty of weight low down, but that was important because it lowered the centre of gravity of what would inevitably be quite a tall vehicle, and so helped the on-road handling and off-road stability.

For some years North American regulations had included some guidelines about low-speed impact damage, stipulating that minor parking knocks should not cause damage to safety-related items such as lights. Some car manufactur-

ers had met these by using 'stroker' bumpers, which were mounted on telescopic struts and would move back in a controlled way under impact before returning to their original position.

The new Range Rover team investigated these at an early stage, but eventually rejected them. Instead, they developed deformable 'crush cans'. These were essentially metal boxes at the front of the chassis behind the bumper, which absorbed impacts in a controlled way and were easily and cheaply replaceable. Land Rover customers first saw them on the revised first-generation Range Rovers and Discoverys introduced in March 1994. On the first-generation Range Rovers, their ends were covered by very visible plastic 'buffers', but on the new model they would be concealed behind the bumper and front apron.

Suspension

Getting the necessary ride quality was not an easy job. During the Project Discovery period, the engineers did investigate an independent front suspension. Meanwhile, they also began to look at ways of decoupling the axles from the bodyshell to improve both ride and refinement, and decided that the most promising option was an air suspension system. Some luxury cars (such as Lincoln in the USA) already had such a system, but it was new to Land Rover and would have to be designed and developed from the ground up.

At one stage, both independent front suspension and air suspension were under investigation together. Engineer Graham Silvers remembered two 'mule' prototypes from around 1990–91 that had both. However, the independent front suspension compromised off-road ability too much, and the tight project deadlines meant that the team had to abandon that line of development and move on. Independent front suspension would have to wait until an advanced electronic control system made all-round independent air suspension feasible for the third-generation Range Rover in 2001. So the suspension engineers now aimed to get better ride refinement by developing lighter beam axles and reducing the weight of other unsprung elements in the suspension.

The great advantage of air suspension was that the vehicle would actually ride on four columns of compressed air, each contained within a rubber bag between the axle and the main structure. Not only would the ride be softer than with traditional steel springs, but the passenger cabin would be quieter because these columns of air would insulate it from road noise.

The new system was developed in conjunction with Dunlop, who already manufactured air suspension systems for trucks and buses. But Land Rover decided to add to it a sophisticated ride-height adjustment system that would allow the vehicle to adapt to a variety of situations. There would be a normal ride height, a slightly lower one to improve handling and aerodynamics at speed, and an ultra-

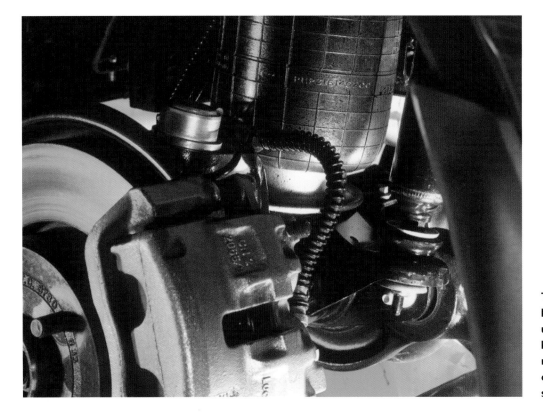

The air suspension, seen here on the front axle, used air-filled rubber bags as the springing medium instead of conventional steel springs.

low one to make embarkation and disembarkation easier from a vehicle which was, after all, quite high off the ground. Then there would be a fourth one to lift the body higher for off-road work, and a fifth one that would push the wheels downwards in search of contact with the ground if the vehicle bellied out and lost traction while off-road.

All this would be controlled by sophisticated electronics, which were again developed in conjunction with an outside supplier. The whole system was a complete departure for Land Rover, and John Hall recognized the risks attached to introducing so much new technology at the same time. So he argued for the air suspension to be incorporated into the existing Range Rover as early as possible, in order to give Land Rover as much experience as possible of the system in service.

It was a good thing that he did. Air suspension was slated for introduction on the existing Range Rover in autumn 1991, but the system failed its final reliability tests that July. A number of vehicles had already been built with it for the press launch, which was promptly cancelled, and it was a further developed version of the system that entered production a year later for the Vogue SE and new long-wheelbase Vogue LSE models. So by the time the new Range Rover was introduced in autumn 1994, air suspension had been in production for two years and Land Rover knew far more about it than they would otherwise have done.

Styling

With their duties on Project Jay coming to an end, the Land Rover styling team were able to make a start on proposals for the new Range Rover during 1988. Their task was never going to be an easy one, not least because it was constrained by existing customer perceptions of what a Range Rover 'should' look like. 'Whatever style we came out with was always going to be controversial,' said John Hall after the launch some years later, his comment accompanied by a wry smile.

It was, and still is, quite common practice in the motor industry to commission a specialist design studio to produce a visual proposal for a new model, and to compare this with the in-house proposals. If nothing else, it ensures that a manufacturer's own design team is not out of step with trends elsewhere. So while the Land Rover stylists were sketching away at their premises in Shirley's Drayton Road, Managing Director Tony Gilroy asked the Italian styling house of Bertone to put forward a proposal for the new Range Rover. Another proposal was commissioned from the celebrated British freelance team of John Heffernan and Ken Greenly. This meant that there would be multiple different proposals, from which the very best could be chosen.

It was probably in the late summer of 1988 that the stylists made a selection of ten different design proposals and

Conventional sill..
No rubbing strip.
Wrap round grille & headlamp.

Flared sill with extra feature.
Rubbing strip.
Non wrap round grille & headlamp.

The Bertone design proposal was quite slick and would have worked well, apart from that very American front-end design.

THEME A

turned them into full-size two-dimensional renderings. These were then lined up for review at Drayton Road – a great barn of a place, which lent itself well to the job. The ten proposals ranged from minimum-change designs that looked much like the existing production model, to more extreme suggestions that included a one-box MPV-like design that dated from 1986 and the time of the Ibex project.

From all these, a provisional selection was agreed; five designs were turned into scale models, and three of those were then turned into full-size 'clays'. Two came from Land

Door lower flared into sill.
Large rubbing strip.
Rear door shutline into wheelarch.

Smaller rubbing strip.
Rear door shutline around wheelarch.

THEME B

Theme B from Land Rover's own design studio was the one selected for development. Details would change, but it was recognizably the ancestor of the production vehicle.

Conventional sill.
Angled stepped waist line.
Round wheelarches.
Upper tailgate shut on rear of vehicle.

Sill has additional finisher onto door.
Radiused waist line.
Squared off wheelarch tops.
Upper tailgate shut on side of vehicle.

THEME C

Two different stepped waistline styles were tried on Theme C, again by Land Rover's own design team.

Rover itself, and the third was the Bertone proposal. They were presented to the Rover Board in October 1988 (the date on documents submitted for the review is 29 October). Bertone's proposal – Theme A in those presented to the Rover Board – had a most American-looking front end, allied to clean lines that were typical of the Italian design house. Themes B and C were by Land Rover's own stylists, with a stepped waistline on Theme C, but it was the less unconventional Theme B that gained the Board's approval.

That final choice of design theme was made while the new Range Rover was still being developed as Project Discovery, and just a few months before it was renamed Project Pegasus. Although the basic shape would not now change, it would be developed in detail by a styling team working under George Thomson, who had been responsible for the styling of the award-winning Discovery. Among the details that would evolve – and cause a great deal of difficulty along the way – was the design of the headlamps (see panel). There was also a change to the roof after the full-size fibreglass styling model had been put alongside a current-production Range Rover for comparison. As stylist Mike Sampson remembers, 'the roof looked too thin' – and so it was raised by 15mm (just over ½in), giving not only better definition to the outside lines, but also bringing extra headroom inside.

An important part of the styling brief for the new model was to ensure that it was instantly recognizable as a Range Rover, and to that end Thomson and his team knew that they would have to retain a number of key styling features, which, according to market research, the public identified as Range Rover characteristics. Among these were the raised outer sections of the bonnet – usually referred to as 'castellations' – and the strong horizontal grille bars. Also important was the so-called 'floating roof', which was created by painting

This full-size model appears to be an earlier version of the Theme C design, without the stepped waistline.

the roof in the body colour but using blacked-out window pillars all round so that the roof appeared to float above the lower body.

While Thomson and his team worked on the detail of the new styling, the basic shape was being tested out at customer clinics. Here, potential buyers of the new vehicle were asked about their requirements in a luxury 4×4, and were then shown a concept sketch of the new Range Rover (which was, of course, not identified as such) and asked for their reactions.

John Hall has admitted that he was very sceptical about these customer clinics. He argued that they tended to lead car makers into a lowest common-denominator mentality, which in turn produced bland cars. However, he remembered two key events from this period, both of them at clinics held in France. On the first occasion, the customers had been asked what they would look for in a luxury 4×4,

Further refinement of the selected theme had reached this stage by December 1989. The rendering was by Mike Sampson.

The body-in-white, a more conventional structure than the one on the original Range Rover.

HEADLAMP DESIGN

The Range Rover design theme chosen for further development at the end of 1988 incorporated rectangular headlamps. These were perfectly in keeping with the overall design theme, but there were concerns within Land Rover that they were a step too far away from the familiar 'face' of the existing Range Rover with its round headlamps. These concerns were well founded: at the 1994 press launch of the second-generation model, several journalists asked why the round lamps had not been retained.

George Thomson had confirmed many years before that the single round lamps did not work well with the new shape. Even though they looked fine in two-dimensional sketches, in practice there were difficulties in integrating them with the rounded front corners of the new vehicle, and from some angles they simply did not look right.

Even so, the design team did look at several alternative headlamp designs before settling on the production style. By late 1988 they were looking at paired round headlamps, one with a 7in (17.8cm) diameter and the other with a 5¾in

A lot of work was done on headlamp design. This was a proposal from late 1988, with 7in (17.8cm) outboard lamps and 5.75in (14.6cm) inboard lamps.

(14.6cm) diameter. During 1989 there were sketches to illustrate paired 5¾in round lamps, paired square lamps (which looked very American in style), and even single round lamps as used on the first-generation Range Rover.

The various alternative headlamp styles remained under investigation into 1990, when the production design was finally settled. Undoubtedly a factor in the retention of the rectangular lamps was that such designs were fashionable at the time, and that using them therefore hinted at use of the latest technology! Even then, there remained an undercurrent of discontent with the design, and it was modified for the 2000 model-year Range Rovers to incorporate blackout 'masks', which gave the impression of two round lamps with different sizes.

and the answers had come up as an almost perfect picture of what Land Rover had in mind for the new Range Rover. So, feeling very pleased with themselves, the Land Rover team presented their concepts of the new vehicle – only to be told that this was definitely not what the customers had in mind! On the second occasion, one potential (French) buyer suggested that the concept had erred too much towards the luxury car and too far from the 4×4. His verdict was more useful, and very memorable: he suggested that Land Rover needed to 'give it some Wellingtons'!

The final styling was signed off in spring 1990, but a few details continued to evolve. Aerodynamic testing, for example, led to a small 'ledge' being added to each E-pillar, just above the waistline, where it supposedly made an important contribution to the Range Rover's stability at speed. The decision to abandon the planned 'stroker' bumpers seems to have been made in this period, too, and it led to further detail changes. Associated adjustments left the top of the rear bumper lower down, and rather less neatly integrated into the lines of the body sides. At the rear, plastic corner fillets were added to disguise the mismatch; the trick is obvious when pointed out, but good enough not to be obvious otherwise.

Interior Design

There had been quite a lot of discussion about making the new Range Rover into a seven-seater during the mid-1980s. People carriers (MPVs, or mini-vans) were becoming increasingly popular, and their use of flexible seating seemed

Early 1989 saw these proposals for rectangular headlamps. A standard production Range Rover of the time was used for comparison purposes.

Yet another proposal with lamps of two different sizes, this one dated from 1989.

The problem had still not been resolved by June 1990, when Mike Samspon sketched up this front end showing single round headlamps, like those of the existing production Range Rover.

A direct comparison: single round and rectangular lamps were tried out on this full-size mock-up.

an attractive trend to follow. It was certainly this thinking that had been behind that radical proposal back in 1986 to style the new Range Rover as a single-box design. However, the people-carrier idea was ruled out after the October 1988 styling review, and the design team settled on a more conventional five-seat estate car approach. Even then, the idea did not go away, and engineers Graham Silvers and Malcolm Ainsley remembered that the project team looked into the possibility of a rearward-facing occasional seat in the load area to increase the number of passengers that could be carried. The idea was abandoned on the grounds that there was not enough room.

The basic interior design came together quite quickly. The stylists' overall aim was to make it as good as the interior of a contemporary luxury saloon, while retaining a distinctive Land Rover character. This meant losing some traditional Land Rover features, and one casualty was the separate transfer box lever. In its place, the stylists proposed an H-gate selector for the automatic gearbox, which eliminated the extra lever and brought the controls for the main and transfer gearboxes together in a more customer-friendly format. The engineers then came up with servo control of the transfer box selector mechanism to make the whole thing possible, and for the manual-gearbox models – which were always expected to be much less popular than automatics – a push-button control on the facia did the job.

△ FEBRUARY 89

ABOVE: **Interior development: these pictures show the state of play in February and May 1989.**

Flowing lines characterized this dashboard proposal by Alan Sheppard in 1989. Note the mobile phone fitted into the centre console behind the handbrake.

Even the automatic gear selector was carefully designed: this proposal was by David Brisbourne in the styling studio.

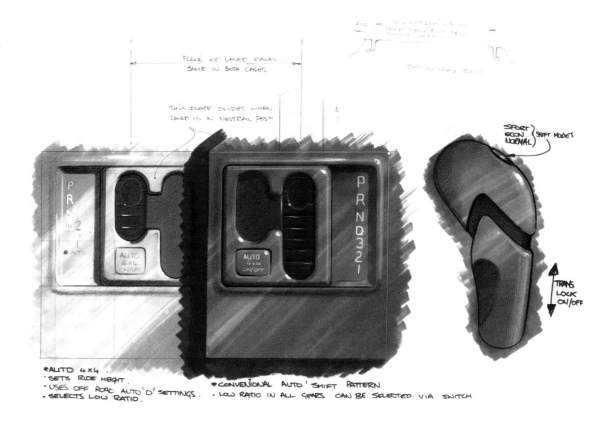

That innovation was an important one, and with it came others that gave the new Range Rover the right sort of high-tech ambience. There was a sophisticated new heating, ventilating and air-conditioning system (see Chapter 2). The instrument display was designed to incorporate an electronic 'message-board', which warned the driver about malfunctions or minor issues such as doors that were not properly shut. All this and many other new features on the vehicle were controlled through an electronic 'brain' called the BECM (Body Electronic Control Module), which was altogether new technology for Land Rover.

Like the exterior styling, the interior design continued to evolve in detail after being approved in principle during 1990. In the beginning, for example, the passenger's side of the facia was designed with an open parcels shelf and a grab handle – though few people ever saw the production version of this because a decision was made to standardize a passenger's side airbag for most markets. George Thomson also remembers that there were some changes in the front seat area: the centre console was slimmed down, the seats were moved inboard slightly, and the steering wheel position was changed to give more thigh room.

Engines – The Petrol Options

Land Rover's assumption from the start was that petrol engines would account for the majority of sales, even though there would be demand for a diesel option as well. In the USA, and in certain other countries where there was no market for diesel engines in luxury cars, petrol engines would be the only option.

The strategy was to offer two different sizes of petrol engine, one for the mid-range models and the other for a flagship model. As Land Rover's own light alloy V8 still had plenty of development life in it, those engines were to be developed from it. Astonishingly, the V8 was already an elderly design, having started life in 1961 with General Motors for that company's compact saloons in the USA. Bought by Rover in 1965 and put into production for Rover cars in 1967, it had been the powerplant of the original Range Rover from the start, and was still highly regarded.

So the engine designers looked at how to develop the engines that the new model would need. The V8 had just been enlarged to a 3.9-litre capacity, which was introduced in 1988 for the USA and in 1989 elsewhere, and with further development could become the standard petrol option. However, several different schemes were considered for the more powerful 'flagship' V8. John Hall remembered that one of these involved developing new cylinder heads with 4 valves per cylinder, twin camshafts and a vastly more complicated camshaft drive arrangement. All the costings were done, but the engine never progressed beyond paper schemes because less complicated and less costly alternatives were found.

Also briefly considered was a supercharged version of the 3.9-litre engine. The plan was to use an Eaton supercharger, and at least one prototype engine was built and tried in a development vehicle. 'The supercharged engine was a lovely, refined unit,' remembered Graham Silvers. 'It would have been a very efficient engine as well, because the extra capacity [adopted for production] wasn't needed.' This engine was tried out in some first-generation Range Rover 'mules', but further development was ruled out on the grounds of cost, weight and likely performance. 'On paper,' explained John Hall, 'supercharging looks very attractive, but it takes so much power to drive it and it increases the heat to water so much that it's really not worth the trip.' The engines team therefore decided to develop a long-stroke version of the 3.9-litre engine, to give a 4.5-litre size.

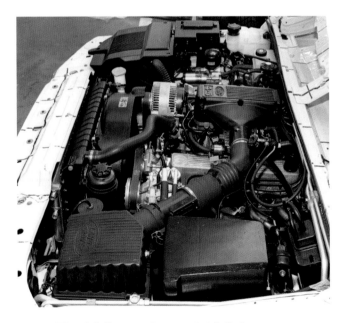

The 4.6-litre engine was initially known as a 4.5-litre, and that name is on the plenum cover of this example, which has been trial fitted into a wooden engine-bay mock-up.

The three engines chosen for the 38A: the 4.0-litre and 4.6-litre V8s are in the foreground, with the 2.5-litre diesel behind.

So a comprehensive engine development programme was drawn up around the 3.9-litre and 4.5-litre sizes. In practice, almost every single component was redesigned or modified, and to identify the new version of the smaller size, Land Rover renamed it a 4.0-litre, even though its 3947cc swept volume was unchanged from that of its predecessor. As for the 4.5-litre, its long stroke gave a swept volume of 4554cc, and about eighteen months before the planned launch of the new Range Rover, the Land Rover marketing team decreed that it should be renamed a 4.6-litre V8, to make it sound as large and impressive as possible.

The revised versions of the V8 were recognizable by their serpentine ancillary drive belt, which simplified the various ancillary drives at the front of the engine and reduced the front-to-rear length by 3in (75mm). This saved valuable space within the engine bay. Further work was done on the injection system, and the sharing of engineering resources with the Rover Group led to the Land Rover engineers choosing the group's GEMS (Generic Engine Management System) electronic control system for both versions of the engine.

Engines – The Diesel

The existing Range Rover had been available with a diesel engine option since 1986, and this accounted for a majority of sales in continental European countries such as France and Italy, where large petrol engines were taxed so heavily as to be almost unsaleable. However, John Hall's 1988 review had highlighted the fact that Land Rover did not have a diesel engine that was refined enough to suit the pretensions of the new Range Rover. There was a new engine on the way – a 4-cylinder direct-injection type that would be announced as

the 200Tdi in 1989 – but the focus of its development was on fuel economy rather than on refinement. It was certainly nowhere near refined enough for the new Range Rover.

So John Bilton, who was the powertrain planner working for Alan Edis in the Product Planning department, set about locating a suitable engine to buy in. He started by arranging for engines from various European manufacturers to be evaluated at Solihull. There were 6-cylinder diesels from Steyr, Mercedes-Benz, VM and BMW, and even a 5-cylinder from Audi, but it was the BMW engine that ended up a clear winner. So Land Rover formally approached the German company to see if they were prepared to supply engines for the forthcoming new Range Rover.

Bilton remembered that BMW were flattered by Land Rover's interest in their engine, but somewhat taken aback when the Solihull engineers told them it would need further development for its Range Rover application. As a saloon car engine, it had not been waterproofed to the standards Land

Another trial fit, this time of the **BMW** diesel engine in an engine bay mock-up.
Many details of the installation would change before production began.

Rover needed, and its oil system had not been designed to work on side slopes. However, once they understood what was needed, the BMW engineers were happy to go ahead.

Land Rover and BMW signed a development contract in late 1989, and the Germans began by putting one of their development engines into a first-generation Range Rover Turbo D. The conversion was carried out at their Steyr factory and was, by all accounts, a great success. So a contract to develop the engine jointly with Land Rover to meet the specific Range Rover requirements and to supply it in quantity for production vehicles was signed not long afterwards, probably in 1990.

Interestingly, the story of Land Rover and that BMW diesel engine can be traced right back to 1981 – many years before work began on the second-generation Range Rover. At that stage, BMW was still developing its new M21 diesel engine, but offered Land Rover a preview to see if it might have any value as a Land Rover engine in the future. John Bilton was their point of contact, but at that stage Land Rover did not need a new diesel engine. So Bilton expressed polite interest and let the contact lapse.

On its introduction in 1983, BMW's 2.4-litre M21 engine gained widespread acclaim as the world's most refined pas-

senger car diesel. By 1986, the German company was working on its replacement, a 2.5-litre with the M51 designation, and a representative visited John Bilton in the UK to see if Land Rover might be interested in looking at this one. Knowing that a new Range Rover was in the offing – although it was then some way away – Bilton kept the relationship warm until Land Rover was ready to look at its diesel engine options in 1988–89. He recalled some years later how the astonishing sales success of the Land Rover Discovery, which became available in autumn 1989, made BMW much more anxious to sell their engine to Land Rover for the new Range Rover!

Transmission

Two things about the transmission were clear from the time of John Hall's review in 1988. First, it would have to offer a low range to give the new Range Rover the off-road ability that set it apart from other luxury cars. Second, both manual and automatic gearboxes would be needed. Most customers would probably choose the automatic, but there was certain to be a proportion of buyers – probably mainly of the less expensive models – who would want a manual.

Two pre-production vehicles were sectioned in Australia and were used to demonstrate the features of the new Range Rover on a nationwide tour. This is one of them: the vehicle has serial number MA300185, and was built in April 1994.

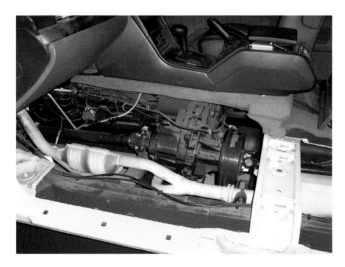

Clear in this view of the sectioned vehicle is that the transfer gearbox is located on the left of the main gearbox. The two exhaust pipes from the V8 engine's manifolds meet here, and one of the catalytic converters is also visible.

This view from further back in the sectioned vehicle shows the main silencer and the area below the rear seat. The removable rear parcels shelf has been stowed in the footwell as a temporary measure.

As far as the low range requirement was concerned, the choice quickly fell on a two-speed transfer gearbox made by Borg Warner. This was introduced first on 1989 models of the first-generation Range Rover, and it had two important advantages over the in-house LT230 design used in other Land Rover models. First, it was silent in operation thanks to its use of a roller chain drive instead of a gear drive; and second, it incorporated a viscous-coupled centre differential that automatically locked the drive between front and rear axles if the wheel rotation speeds differed by more than a predetermined amount. So the risk of driver error in failing to lock a manual centre differential was removed, which added to the ease of driving what was, after all, to be a luxury 4×4 vehicle.

Traditionally, the transfer box in Land Rovers was located on the right-hand side of the primary gearbox, an arrangement that made for a rather cramped toebox in the first-generation Range Rover. So for the new model, the transmission engineers decided to relocate it on the left. This meant that the new Range Rover would also need new axles, because all existing production types had their differentials on the right to suit the usual position of the transfer box. Bizarrely, however, the Range Rover remained the only Land Rover product with this arrangement. As a result, putting the 4.6-litre engine and its accompanying transmission into the 2003 Discovery Series II became more complicated than

it would otherwise have been. The installation had to be re-engineered to use an uprated LT230 transfer box mounted on the right to suit the right-hand mounting of the Discovery's differentials.

There was no such difficulty over the choice of automatic gearbox, because the German-built ZF 4HP22 type in the existing Range Rover would remain ideal for the job. Even the additional torque from the new 4.6-litre engine was not a problem, because ZF offered a stronger version, called the 4HP24. The German company had also been developing its gearbox control systems to remain in the forefront of design, and both versions of the ZF gearbox would be available with a selectable dual-mode control system, which gave 'sport' up-changes (by holding on to the lower gears until the engine reached higher revs) as an alternative to the standard settings.

As for the manual gearbox, the development team decided that they wanted a better gearbox than the five-speed LT77 that was offered in the existing Range Rover. So they came to an arrangement with Borg Warner, who designed a new five-speed gearbox specially for the Range Rover. Land Rover engineer Malcolm Ainsley remembered the prototypes as being 'very nice, with a lovely change', but the project was cancelled, possibly on cost grounds.

That left the only choice as a new gearbox that was being developed within the Rover Group, which became the R380 when it entered production in early 1994. The R stood for Rover, and the 380 represented its torque capacity of 380Nm (about 280lb/ft). At least one of these was built into a 4.6-litre Range Rover prototype, and Malcolm Ainsley remembered that on one occasion this achieved 140mph (225km/h) downhill on a German autobahn. However, he also remembered that the combination of 4.6-litre V8 and R380 gearbox was not a success: the big V8 'tended to destroy them'! This may partially explain why no manual gearbox was made available with the 4.6-litre engine when the new Range Rover entered production, although the official explanation that there was no demand for a manual gearbox at the top end of the market was also undoubtedly true.

THE PROTOTYPES

Various components destined for the new Range Rover had been tried out in 'mule' prototypes – engineering hacks that were modified first-generation Range Rovers. Probably the last of these had the new, long-wheelbase-chassis, under-stretched, first-generation Range Rover bodies, and began testing in late 1990 or early 1991.

The first recognizable prototypes of what was now the Project 38A vehicle were completed by October 1991, according to John Hall. These were known as 'DO1' types, and were representative of the finished article both visually and in terms of the overall package, although there were many details that had still not been signed off for production and were therefore not yet present. The panels for these vehicles were mainly made on prototype tooling, which can be produced quickly at relatively low cost but also wears out quite quickly. Other items on them were hand produced.

Land Rover went to considerable trouble to prevent pictures of these prototypes from reaching the public, and had the Styling Department draw up a special kit of GRP disguise panels. These panels were first used when the DO1 prototypes went out on test in the last quarter of 1991, and *AutoBild* in Germany, and *Auto Express* and *Car* magazines in Britain, all managed to publish pictures of the disguised vehicles testing in California's Death Valley before the end of the year. However, the disguise did its job, and the only thing that the pictures revealed was that the new model bore some resemblance to the old and was very big!

'There were two levels of disguise,' remembered Graham Silvers, 'one with just GRP panels and the second with a

canvas hood.' The kits were actually made by MGA Panels, near Coventry, but there was only one complete kit with the hood as well. Graham Silvers also remembered that 'The disguise was a pain to use, and didn't help with things like noise tests.' And on one occasion disguised Range Rovers got the team into a sticky situation. Some of them were using disguised prototypes for squeak and rattle tests in Galway, a remote and sparsely populated area in the west of Ireland. Unfortunately, these rather unusual-looking vehicles attracted the attention of a local IRA terrorist unit,

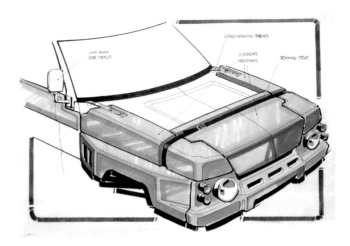

The disguise cladding was drawn up by Land Rover's stylists: this is one of the renderings for the front-end cladding.

The overall aim of the disguise panels was to make the prototypes look like military trucks from a distance. They did the job, but the development team hated using them!

and one day the team found themselves stopped by an IRA roadblock. As a result, remembered Graham Silvers, 'we pulled testing out of Ireland!'

Realizing that the disguise panels were probably more trouble than they were worth, the team changed tack. 'After that,' said John Hall, 'we generally drove [the prototypes] in a fairly drab colour, looking slightly tatty ... and you get very little attention at all!' In fact, even though the test vehicles continued to do a lot of road work in Scotland and elsewhere, no more photographs appeared in the press until autumn 1993, when *Carweek* newspaper caught an undisguised red vehicle at a test track somewhere and published a front-page story in its issue dated 8 September.

There were still some major challenges facing the engineers during this phase of the 38A Range Rover's development in the early 1990s. Crash safety performance had to be monitored through a series of barrier-impact tests, while exhaust emissions had to be kept down to the required levels. European and North American regulations in both these areas were very different, which complicated the engineers' task. Also important was to design for anticipated tightening of the existing regulations, so that changes in legislation during the production life of the vehicle would not present major problems.

John Hall remembered that achieving the required levels of overall vehicle refinement was one of the biggest challenges of all. The main work on this began at some time in the first half of 1993, by which point the 38A team was also having to make some far-reaching decisions. Some of the features they had planned (such as the 'dribble-wipe': *see* box) had to be abandoned at the last minute, either because

they were not ready or because the cost accountants intervened. Others were shelved for use on future upgrades. So the engineers remained busy right to the end.

Pilot production began at the end of 1993, even though the launch was not planned to take place until autumn 1994. Records suggest that just nine vehicles were built that year, but production was gradually ramped up over the first half of 1994, and volume production started in July. By the time of the media launch in September, more than 1,000 examples of the new Range Rover had been built, and production rates were increasing steadily.

Looking very down at heel, and probably deliberately so to avoid attracting attention, two of the development prototypes were pictured at Solihull in August 1995, just before the global launch. The green one is G437 RCW and the grey one is J102 WAX.

Production vehicle number 35 – strictly a pre-production model despite its production chassis number – is the oldest survivor; it now belongs to the Dunsfold Collection.

THE 'DRIBBLE-WIPE'

Right up until the last minute, the new Range Rover was to be launched with a 'dribble-wipe' feature. This gave a delayed single sweep of the windscreen wipers after they had been switched off, to catch the dribble of water that always runs down the screen from the top of the wipers' arc.

However, although Land Rover service personnel were trained to expect this in advance of the launch, the feature was deleted on cost grounds, and never reappeared in the 38A specification.

Prototype and Development Vehicles

Land Rover probably built several hundred prototypes of the second-generation Range Rover, but very little has so far been discovered about them. Just three have been identified:

G437 RCW LHD, painted flat mid-green; three-spoke wheels
G248 YNB LHD, painted white; probably a 4.6 HSE
J102 WAX RHD, painted flat light grey; three-spoke wheels

In addition, pre-production model number 35, built in January 1994, survives in the Dunsfold Collection. Painted silver-grey and specified as a TL3 (4.6 HSE) model, it has a number of non-production features, and the trim seems to have been completed with non-matching colours. The engine plenum cover reads '4.5' instead of the production '4.6'. This vehicle is thought to have been used for heater and interior assessment for the Australian market, despite the LHD configuration. Its chassis number of J4KA300035 decodes as follows:

J   4.6-litre high-compression V8 with catalyst
4   LHD automatic
K   1993 specification
A   Built at Solihull
300035   Serial number

CHANGES OF OWNERSHIP (2)

In January 1994, the German BMW company bought the Rover Group (which included Land Rover) from British Aerospace. Negotiations had been conducted in such secrecy and with such speed that the announcement came as a surprise even to senior executives within the two companies.

When the new Range Rover was announced at the end of September 1994 with a BMW diesel among its engine options, there was a rash of uninformed speculation about the extent of BMW's involvement in the project.

The fact is that the new Range Rover was ready to enter production (bar a few last-minute issues) before the BMW take-over was concluded. It was therefore far too late for the German company to make any major changes, and in practice the BMW Board simply rubber-stamped the proposal to put the new model into production. The engine supply contract had of course been drawn up some three years earlier, before there was any question of BMW buying the Rover Group.

CHAPTER TWO

EARLY DAYS, 1995–1997

Introducing the new Range Rover was a very important event for both Land Rover and the Rover Group as a whole. Not only was the 38A the most expensive Land Rover ever made, it was also to be the Rover Group's new flagship model, offering more luxury than any of the cars that wore Rover badges at the time. Although it was undoubtedly a Land Rover, with all the legendary off-road ability which that implied, it was also intended to poach sales from conventional luxury cars such as the Mercedes S-Class, BMW 7-Series or Lexus luxury saloons. And that was a very tall order indeed.

So the public launch was a deliberately ambitious affair, quite radical in concept and designed to make potential Range Rover owners feel part of an exclusive group. The event was timed for the weekend of Friday 30 September to Sunday 2 October, a few days in advance of the new model's formal global unveiling at the Paris Motor Show on

Tuesday 4 October, and a few days after the press embargo was lifted at midnight on 28 September. Participating dealers around the world invited existing and potential Range Rover customers into their showrooms, where they were able to see an example of the new model and to watch a series of special video programmes about it.

The twist was that several of these special programmes were broadcast 'live' to TV screens in the dealerships via a dedicated satellite link. Land Rover Live, as it was called, featured a series of events around the world in which new Range Rovers enabled a number of prominent personalities to take part in activities and adventures that were held in Japan, Patagonia, Botswana, Vermont, Madrid and the Cotswolds. Each of these events was designed to dramatize one of the Land Rover marque values of the day: these were individualism, authenticity, freedom, adventure, guts and supremacy. It was all very carefully conceived, slickly

The first production example of the new Range Rover was a 4.0 SE, and was handed over to the Heritage Collection at Gaydon. It was pictured here during the event that celebrated sixty-five years of the Land Rover marque in 2013.

This Australian publicity picture shows very well the appeal of the Range Rover's driving position. The model is a 4.6 HSE.

presented, and very effective in getting the message out to a very wide audience.

Meanwhile, the media had already been briefed about the new model, at a lavish event held during August and September. The venue was Cliveden, a stately home in Buckinghamshire, which had become a hotel and conference centre. Formerly the home of Lord and Lady Astor, it had acquired a certain notoriety during the early 1960s as the venue for a party where society prostitute Christine Keeler had met various clients – among them, the Defence Minister John Profumo.

The launch event lasted for several weeks, as the media representatives of one nation after another took their turns to drive the new models. They arrived in the afternoon, got their first look at a new Range Rover just before dinner, and then spent most of the next day trying the vehicles out. There was an interesting road route laid out, taking in both Buckinghamshire and Oxfordshire, but it was perhaps significant that there was only a very limited off-road demonstration course. Land Rover knew very well that not many first buyers of these luxury machines would be using them very seriously in rough terrain, despite their undoubted off-road capabilities.

By this stage, volume production had of course begun at Solihull. Most of the first production models were intended for customers in the UK, although there were certainly some early sample vehicles with the specifications planned for other countries. The plan was to roll out the new model across all its intended markets in phases, and Range Rovers for continental Europe, the Far East and South America would be the first overseas examples in the final quarter of 1994. Sales in Africa, Australia, Canada, Eastern Europe, Japan, the USA and the United Arab Emirates would follow in spring 1995. Of these countries, the USA was unquestionably the largest and therefore the most important potential market, and the story of the NAS (North American specification) Range Rovers has a chapter to itself later on in this book.

PRE-PRODUCTION AND PRESS LAUNCH VEHICLES

Pre-Production Models

A few very early pre-production vehicles were registered during the 1994 registration year (August 1993 to July 1994) and therefore had L-prefix registration plates. Some were probably lent to privileged Land Rover contacts, while others went to major magazines whose opinions were considered important in shaping buyer perceptions of the new Range Rover.

Several of these were registered by the authorities in Bath; it was standard Land Rover practice to register prototype and pre-production vehicles well away from the Birmingham area to deflect attention when they were out on the roads. All four so far identified were also in dark colours, which made them less likely to stand out and attract attention. They were:

L5 LGL   Avalon Blue 4.0 SE, lent to *Autocar*.

L6 LGL   Dark-coloured 2.5 DSE pictured in *Diesel Car* for September 1999.

L9 RGL   Avalon Blue 4.6 HSE, tested for *Carweek* of 29 September 1994.

L10 RGL   Epsom Green 4.6 HSE, tested for *Land Rover Owner* magazine in its November 1994 issue; also pictured in *Car* magazine for November 1994.

Other vehicles were given London registrations, again no doubt to deflect attention from their Midlands origins. Those so far identified were:

M38 RHV   Portofino Red 4.6 HSE, photographed at Cliveden for the launch press release.

M39 RHV   Avalon Blue 2.5 DSE; pictured in *Autocar,* 28 September 1994, and *Carweek,* 29 September 1994.

M40 RHV   Sahara Gold 4.0 SE; appeared in some press release pictures.

Press-Launch Models

The early production vehicles used on the press launch at Cliveden during August and September 1994 were registered in the M-CVC series, a Coventry issue. The M-CVC vehicles also appeared in most of the press launch photographs. It looks as if a very large quantity of M-CVC numbers was allocated to Land Rover, as they were used on many factory-registered vehicles during 1994. However, the ones allocated to the 38A press fleet were all in the 200 number range. The lowest number identified is M201 CVC (a 2.5 DT in Alpine White), and the highest is M289 CVC (a blue 4.6 HSE).

The new Range Rover of course had superb off-road ability. This is a pre-production model, **M40 RHV**, finished in Sahara Gold. The grey bumpers were universal at this stage, but are easier to see on lighter coloured vehicles like this one.

The press launch vehicles were registered in the **M-CVC** series: this is **M270 CVC**, a 4.6 **HSE** model that was also the first 38A the author ever drove. NICK DIMBLEBY

Like its predecessor, the 38A had a horizontally split tailgate; the lower section made an ideal grandstand seat at outdoor events. NICK DIMBLEBY

The rectangular headlamps were a controversial feature from the start. Each light unit actually contained two lamps, and on the higher specification models there was a wash-wipe system as well. NICK DIMBLEBY

With the two sections of the split rear seat folded forwards, the new Range Rover provided an immense load space.

Other M-CVC 38A Range Rovers played important roles in the early days of the model. There were probably ten white vehicles allocated to the Land Rover Experience demonstration team (thought to be M601 CVC to M610 CVC), while M751–753, 761–762 and 774 CVC all became police demonstrators.

THE 1995 MODELS

Every new 1995 model Range Rover shared a basic specification that included air suspension, ABS, side impact beams in the doors and a remotely activated anti-theft system, but there was a wide variety of differences beyond that. Even the fitting of twin airbags was not universal: some countries, including South Africa, took their first 38A models without any airbags at all. In such cases, there was an open parcels shelf on the passenger's side, with a grab handle in front of it.

Electric windows were standard on all models, and always came with both a 'one-shot down' feature and an anti-trap mechanism, which sensed an obstruction when the windows were being raised, and shut off the power (mainly to prevent children getting their fingers trapped). The two front door windows also had a 'one-shot up' feature, allowing a single press of the switch to power the window fully closed. Front doors also incorporated puddle lamps in their bottom edges, which illuminated the ground below when the doors were opened. Electrically adjustable door mirrors were standard equipment, too.

There was a non-airbag specification for some overseas markets, shown here on an early South African SE model. The steering-wheel centre is similar to the standard type, but does not carry SRS ('supplemental restraint system') identification.

In order to simplify production, Land Rover developed three standard levels of trim and equipment. These remained essentially constant everywhere the model was sold, although the model names that were applied were not the same in every country. They were known as Trim Levels 1, 2 and 3 (usually abbreviated to TL1, TL2 and TL3 in company documents), and in Britain they corresponded to the entry-level models, the mid-range SE and the flagship HSE variants respectively. The SE letters were generally understood to stand for 'special equipment', but the meaning of HSE has always been more elusive. Even the Land Rover press office did not know when asked in 1995, and suggested that the designation might mean 'higher than SE'!

For convenience, models are generally described by their British designations in the rest of this book, although the American line-up had some important differences from the start: these are explained in Chapter 5.

The Entry-Level Models

The entry-level models (Trim Level 1) were known as the 4.0 and 2.5 DT respectively. They could be had with either a five-speed manual or a four-speed automatic gearbox, although there were no automatic diesels for the 1995 model-year.

These models came with metallic paint as standard, although solid colours were a no-cost option. They were easily recognized in standard form by their distinctly unexciting three-spoke alloy wheels – even designer George Thomson thought they were disappointing – which had a style similar to that used on first-generation Range Rovers from mid-1981. If they had been painted like their predecessors, they might have looked more attractive, but they had

There were never any steel wheels for the 38A models. The entry-level three-spoke alloy design was similar to a design used on the first-generation models from mid-1981, and is seen here on a German market diesel Range Rover.

The entry-level specification featured cloth seats and, as in this case, a manual gearbox. NICK DIMBLEBY

The steering-wheel angle could be adjusted manually by releasing a lever on the column shroud. There were electrically adjustable door mirrors, and a radio-cassette system with ten FM pre-sets – five for MW and five for LW.

The Mid-Range Models

The mid-range models were known as SE types (with the 4.0-litre V8) or DSE types (with the diesel engine). The V8 could be had with both a manual and an automatic gearbox, but the diesel came with only the manual gearbox for 1995.

The front seats were manually adjusted on entry-level and SE models.

a plain metal finish that somehow looked too cheap to suit a Range Rover. Like all wheels on the 1995 Range Rovers, they had a 16in diameter; the rims were 7in wide, and they were supplied with 235/70 R 16 radial tyres.

These were the only versions of the new Range Rover to have fabric upholstery, which had an appearance that even Land Rover documents described as 'towelling'. Burr walnut wood trim was confined to the dashboard and the centre console around the gear lever, and only the driver's seat had height adjustment. This was achieved with a manual lever on the outboard edge of the seat base. The heater allowed driver and passenger to select different temperatures for each side of the passenger compartment, and incorporated a programmed de-mist setting, which put all the available heat on to the windscreen for optimum demisting in cold conditions.

With the SE specification came leather upholstery, but there was still no wood on the door trims. This is the interior of a 1996 2.5 DSE with automatic gearbox. NICK DIMBLEBY

The mid-range models had the five-spoke alloy wheel design as seen here. This is a 1996 2.5 DSE automatic, and a close look shows the air intake grille on the left of the front apron that was unique to these models; it fed cold air to the oil cooler. It also meant that fog lights could not be fitted.

NICK DIMBLEBY

The SE designation had been used for the top models of the first-generation Range Rover, and the fact that there was now a designation above it reflected Land Rover's hopes that the public would perceive the new Range Rover as a step up from the old. However, the SE and DSE models of the 38A were not as well equipped as the old Range Rover Vogue SE (commonly referred to simply as the 'SE'), and this led to some confusion.

The SE and DSE had their own style of alloy wheels, usually called five-hole or DBL types, with 7in rims, and 237/70 R 16 tyres. They also had a removable 'bib' extension to the front apron spoiler (it only needed to be removed for off-road use), and a headlamp wash-wipe system was standard. Tailgate badges read '4.0 SE' or '2.5 DSE'.

These models came with leather upholstery, featuring three broad pleats running front to rear on the seat backs and cushions. Both front seats were electrically heated, although adjustment was still manual. There was a heated windscreen, and cruise-control buttons on the steering wheel. The column stalks operated a trip computer, which included a speed warning chime: drivers could set this to the local speed limit and it would interact with the electronic speedometer to chime a warning if the vehicle exceeded that limit.

Then there was a sophisticated fully automatic heating and air-conditioning system instead of the simple heater on entry-level models. Generally known as the HEVAC (heating, ventilating and air conditioning), this again allowed different settings for the passenger and the driver side. Operation was simple: once a temperature had been selected on the digital readout, the system would achieve and retain that

Tailgate lettering was in the same style for all models.

temperature by using the heater or the air conditioning as necessary. The programmed de-mist feature also brought the heated windscreen into operation to speed up the work of the HEVAC. Unsurprisingly, there was also a better quality radio-cassette system than in the entry-level Range Rovers.

The Flagship Models

The top specification was only available with the 4.6-litre engine, and that in turn was available only with the automatic gearbox. So the flagship model during the 1995 model-year was a 4.6 HSE.

The HSE models had the same detachable bib spoiler as the SE types, and had distinctive five-spoke Stratos alloy wheels with 8in rims that carried wider 255/65 R 16 radial tyres. The flagship Range Rover also had fog lamps in the front apron spoiler (other models had blanking panels), front and rear mudflaps, and an electric sunroof.

The upholstery was leather, of course, and the burr walnut wood extended to the tops of the door trims as well. The steering wheel was also leather trimmed, and incorporated switches for the cruise control and ICE systems. Both front seats had power adjustment, and the driver's seat had a two-position memory. There was also a 'lazy seat' function, which adjusted the driver's seat to a pre-set position by recognizing which of the two ignition keys was being used.

The door mirrors incorporated heating elements that were activated with the heated windscreen. The passen-

The 4.6 HSE was the only model that featured a wood trim insert on the door trims. Also clear on this 1996 model is the dark piping on the Ash Grey leather seats.

SOME PERSONAL REFLECTIONS

I was one of the members of the press invited to the Range Rover launch at Cliveden, and I attended the rotation held over the two days of 11 and 12 August 1994.

I drove two examples, sharing the driving with Mike Hallett of *Off-Road & Four-Wheel Drive* magazine. The first was a green 4.6 HSE, M270 CVC; the second was a red diesel, M204 CVC. As a committed Range Rover owner already, I was quite excited to discover what improvements Land Rover had been able to make for its new model.

I was impressed by the refinement of the new diesel engine, and impressed by the effortless performance of the 4.6-litre model too. But I came away from the launch feeling slightly underwhelmed. Something was missing.

For me, the overall impression was that the second-generation Range Rover was bland. It was trying so hard to be a luxury car that it seemed to have lost some of the rawness and edge that made a Land Rover a proper Land Rover. I was also deeply disappointed by the styling, although it has grown on me since. In fact, the whole vehicle has grown on me since 1994 – but it was not until I tried some of the much improved models of the early 2000s, when the model was just about to be replaced, that I really came to appreciate it for what it was.

ger's side mirror dipped automatically when reverse gear was selected, to help the driver see better along the vehicle's opposite flank. This, though, was just one of a whole selection of electrical convenience features that were unique to the HSE at this stage. Puddle lamps in the rear doors matched the standard front pair, and footwell lamps front and rear turned on when the doors were opened. There was a self-dimming rear-view mirror, the mirror in the pas-senger's side sun visor had a light that came on automatically when it was uncovered, and there were reading lamps mounted high up on the rear pillars.

Finally, the high-line radio-cassette player also controlled a six-disc CD changer, and the lid of the centre cubby box could be reversed to provide cupholders for the front seat passengers – an item designed to please North American customers.

The least powerful of the engine options was the **BMW** turbocharged diesel. It retained prominent **BMW** identification – not least because **BMW** owned Land Rover by this stage.

The mid-range engine was the 4.0-litre V8, here probably in pre-production model M40 RHV.

The most powerful engine option was the 225bhp 4.6-litre petrol V8.

The two V8 engines looked identical under the bonnet, so their size was displayed on the plenum cover.

HIGH SECURITY SYSTEM

The second-generation Range Rover was developed with a highly sophisticated anti-theft system, featuring remote-control engine immobilization and central locking with deadlocks and a rolling code system, plus a four-track ignition and door key instead of the usual two-track type. Several electronic components on each vehicle also stored the VIN, and there were hidden VIN labels and recorded harness labels. All this made identifying a stolen vehicle or its components much easier. In 1996–1997 the Range Rover received at least three high-profile awards in the UK for the excellence of its security features.

Two of these awards came from *What Car?* magazine. On the first occasion, in the August 1996 Security Test, a 4.0-litre was the outright winner. It took the magazine's professional 'car thief' more than two minutes to gain entry to the vehicle, and he needed more than five minutes to drive the vehicle away. On the second occasion, the September 1997 issue of the magazine announced that a 4.0 SE model had come equal first with the then-new Jaguar XK8.

In February 1997, the Range Rover also won the Executive Luxury category of the BVLRA's Vehicle Security Awards.

On Sale

Sales of the new Range Rover were quite exceptional from the start. The original plan had been to build up production gradually to reach the maximum assembly line capacity of 620 vehicles a week thirty months after the launch. In practice, demand was so strong (buoyed up in particular by the North American launch in late spring 1995) that the line was already working at full capacity by November 1995 – just thirteen months after the launch!

Those 1995 models were available in a range of fourteen colours, and there were two interior colours on offer. The entry-level and SE models could be kitted out with some of the items available on more expensive variants at extra cost, and there was a selection of fifty accessories available from the launch date; these included such things as side steps, A-frame bars, bull bars, light protection grilles, roof-rack

The arrival of 18in alloy wheels was driven by customer demand. These are Mondial wheels, clearly inspired by a Ferrari design, and seen here on a 1997 US-market 4.6-litre model. (The body-colour front apron was not yet available on Range Rovers for other markets.)

Interior trims were rather sombre for the first year, but for 1996 a Lightstone Beige option was added, shown here in an SE model.

NERVOUSNESS

Land Rover had been understandably nervous about the introduction of the second-generation Range Rover. Not only was it a huge step forwards in terms of complexity and sophistication, but it was also being introduced to a strongly conservative group of buyers who in many cases were quite passionate about their existing first-generation models. There was a real risk that this group of buyers might reject the new model.

So to retain buyer loyalty, Land Rover had kept the older model in low-volume production when the new one was launched in 1994, a strategy that allowed a longer period for existing Range Rover owners to become used to the new model and to accept it. In fact the new Range Rover, which had been renamed the Range Rover Classic, received such widespread acceptance that production of the old model was closed down in February 1996.

systems, seat covers, and so on. Although very high prices had been predicted in some areas of the press, the new Range Rovers were in fact not a lot more expensive than the models they replaced – a welcome surprise that probably helped initial sales more than a little.

Unfortunately, these first Range Rovers were far from perfect in many cases. They were much more complex vehicles than most of the Solihull assembly line staff had worked on before, and they demanded different attitudes to the assembly process. Training in techniques was all very well, but Land Rover had just taken a huge step in terms of the complexity of its products, and had not realized how much of a difference this might make on the assembly lines. Assembly faults were only a part of the problem, of course, and poor quality components arriving from some of the company's outside suppliers were supposedly to blame for many electrical faults that showed up.

Land Rover's new owners at BMW were deeply unimpressed, and instructed the British company to put its house in order. So Operation Achilles was set up to rectify build faults at dealerships when early 38A Range Rovers came in for routine attention. Their owners probably never realized what had been done to them. Inevitably, news of the quality problems did leak out to the buying public, but it would be some time before Land Rover had identified all the weak-

nesses and had begun to tackle them. In the meantime, more damage was being done: a marketing document produced in 1998 looked back ruefully on the early days of the 38A and reported 'the effect that questionable quality has had on marketplace perceptions has been a painful lesson for Land Rover'.

THE 1996 MODELS

There was never any chance that the 1996 models would be very different from their predecessors. Land Rover's strategy was to keep its engineers on standby to deal with any major problems that were identified through customer feedback. So a few features that had been ready in time for the launch were held over for the 1996 model-year to ensure there would be something new to look at in the showrooms.

As a result, the 1996 model-year was distinguished by only a few novelties. The automatic gearbox became available for diesel models, and there were a few changes to the paint options. The biggest change was that the original two interior colours (Granite Grey and Saddle Tan) were joined by two more. These were Ash Grey (available in both cloth and leather) and Lightstone Beige (available only in leather), lighter colours apparently selected to meet demand in the North American market. At the same time, the restricted colour combinations available in the 1995 model-year gave way to an unfettered choice for customers: all interior colours could now be had with all exterior colours – though there was no doubt that some combinations worked better than others.

All these changes were introduced when the 1996 models were shown to the public at the Frankfurt Motor Show in September 1995. But Land Rover had not finished yet: shortly afterwards, a new 18in alloy wheel called the Mondial became available as an option for the HSE models. At about the same time, a second 18in design called Triple Sport became available through Land Rover Parts as an accessory fit – but to protect LRP's sales, it was never made available as a line-fit option. These new wheels had been called for by Land Rover's Marketing Department, who were somewhat envious of BMW's wide range of alloy wheel options! The designers were delighted to comply, remembered George Thomson, because the larger wheel diameter suited the vehicle's proportions very well. The five-spoke Mondial design was also particularly attractive, making clear

The French 25th Anniversary special edition was probably the first one to have the new Triple Sport alloy wheels. Just visible here are the gold decal side stripes and identifying badge on the rear wing.

that Land Rover was ready and willing to progress beyond the lacklustre entry-level and mid-range wheel designs.

Even though quality control issues continued to dog the new Range Rover during the 1996 model-year, strong sales made it quite clear that it had been enthusiastically accepted. There were, of course, some minor niggles: the vehicle looked much better in light or bright colours than in some of the darker shades, when it looked distinctly slab-sided unless fitted with the HSE-style bodyside rubbing-strips incorporating a bright metal highlight. The wheel styles used on the entry-level and mid-range models remained a disappointment, and the vehicle did look uncomfortably tall

and narrow from behind. But with an enlightened choice from the options list, a 1996 Range Rover could certainly be made to look like the prestigious, desirable mode of transport that its designers had always intended. And above all, most of its new owners were very happy with what they had bought.

A French Special Edition

Land Rover's French National Sales Company had a long track record of using special editions to boost sales, and

With front bull bar (essential in the outback), spare wheel on the roof and decals on the doors, this is one of the Calvert Centenary Expedition Range Rovers. NICK DIMBLEBY

The Calvert Centenary Expedition vehicles, in typical Australian scenery. NICK DIMBLEBY

The 1996 State Review vehicle was pictured here with its two Range Rover predecessors; the 1975 vehicle is on the right, and the 1989 one on the left.

in 1996 they released the first ever special edition of the Range Rover 38A. This was called the 25th Anniversary edition.

As the original Range Rover was introduced in 1970, the model's twenty-fifth anniversary was actually in 1995. However, Land Rover were quite flexible about dates, allowing marketing to take precedence. The US model 25th Anniversary edition was released in 1994, and the UK edition in 1995, both being based on the first-generation model. So 1996 was near enough when the French wanted a special edition of the new Range Rover.

It is not clear how many of these were built, but they were almost certainly created 'in territory' by the French NSC from otherwise standard production models. They were painted in Aspen Silver with a gold coachline, and had a 25th Anniversary decal on each rear wing. Triple Sport alloy wheels from the accessories list were standard. These special-edition models were probably available with either the 2.5-litre diesel engine or the 4.0-litre petrol V8.

An HSE in China

In the mid-1990s, the Rover Group struck a new deal for the supply of vehicles to China, a market that had for many years been denied to Western motor manufacturers. To celebrate the signing of the deal, a Range Rover 4.6 HSE – then the most expensive model in the Rover Group stable – was presented to the Palace Museum in May 1996. It was to be used to transport VIPs and civic dignitaries.

The Calvert Centenary Expedition

Between May and June 1996, Land Rover provided four Range Rovers as transport for the Calvert Centenary Expedition in Western Australia. Organized with the support of the Royal Geographical Society, this 2,400-mile (3,860km) expedition set out to retrace the steps of the ill-fated but heroic scientific Calvert Expedition of 1896.

Although the expedition was a success in scientific terms, it was less of a success for Land Rover. Costs quickly escalated out of control, and it is said that the heads of at least two of the Land Rover Public Relations staff involved in the exercise were made to roll immediately afterwards.

The State Review Range Rover

Land Rover had provided two specially converted first-generation Range Rovers to the British royal family for use as State Review vehicles, following a line of similarly converted Land Rovers that went right back to 1953. The State Review vehicles provided an open driving compartment and an open standing area in the rear, from where the Queen or another senior royal personage could acknowledge crowds or review troops while being driven at state occasions.

In 1996, Land Rover provided a new State Review Range Rover to replace the first one, which had been in use since 1975 and was subsequently withdrawn from service. The new vehicle was of course based on the latest 38A. It was built by LRSV, and was painted in the traditional Royal Claret.

Prototcol prevented LRSV from building exact copies for other rulers, although it is beyond doubt that some asked.

It does appear that similar (but not identical) vehicles were delivered to Oman and Bahrain in the later 1990s; the Omani vehicle was supposedly finished in desert camouflage paint.

THE 1997 MODELS

Land Rover appeared to be very much marking time with its Range Rover at the start of the 1997 model-year. The new season's models were announced at the British International Motor Show in October 1996, but they did not bring any major changes.

The biggest change was in fact to the exhaust systems. To meet the latest European drive-by noise regulations, Land Rover had fitted twin exhaust outlets on every model. It had not been possible to fit larger silencers to meet the new regulations, and so the solution had been to route half the exhaust gases through an additional silencer. This made for some minor alterations to the advertised power and torque outputs of the diesel engine (though not to those of the two petrol V8s), but its main effect for the customers was to increase the cost of a replacement exhaust system. Of course the twin exhaust exits under the rear bumper also became a recognition feature of the 1997 and later models.

WHAT THE PRESS THOUGHT

Solihull always knew that there was no point in making it the fastest and the best if it didn't look like a Range Rover should. Our view is that they have achieved this first objective remarkably well, using powerful cues to underline the relationship.

The performance is acceptable if you use all of the firmly sprung accelerator's long travel… What the 4.0 does beautifully is cruise: this machine will glide along at a true 100mph [160km/h] with no vibration and 3,700rpm showing on the tacho.

The ride is okay on motorways, but pretty lumpy (albeit quiet and well damped) over broken bitumen. But if … you're prepared to judge it against other civilized off-roaders, then it goes instantly to the top of the class.

Refined though it is, the Range Rover cannot compete with the best saloons in outright luxury. – (*Autocar*, 5 October 1994)

The 4.0 SE returned an alarming 17mpg [16.6ltr/100km] in our hands, while the 4.6HSE recorded an even more shameful 15mpg [18.8ltr/100km]. The diesel [managed] 22.6mpg [12.5ltr/100km] overall, with a best of 27mpg [10.5ltr/100km] while touring.

In a vehicle of this size and weight, the diesel's torque looks limp compared with the V8's… – (*Autocar*, 9 November 1994)

If you drive the [automatic DSE] Range Rover hard it feels quite quick, with crisp up-changes, but if you're driving more gently it can feel curiously unresponsive… what it really needs is a bigger, beefier turbodiesel engine, in the same size league as the 4.0 and 4.6 petrol options. That applies even more to the automatic.

Despite the Range Rover's sophisticated air suspension, it still doesn't feel as immediately reassuring on a twisty road as a car. There's a slightly vague, wandering feel to the steering. – (*Diesel Car*, March 1996)

Three new paint colours were introduced to freshen the range, but these replaced three older colours, so the total of fourteen paint options remained the same. Locking wheel nuts were also fitted as standard across the range – perhaps because the more attractive 18in alloy wheels introduced at the end of 1995 had become more of a temptation to thieves.

Although it was largely 'business as usual' with the mainstream Range Rovers for 1997, Land Rover did use the 1996 Motor Show to announce the introduction of an Auto-biography custom-finishing service. The first deliveries of these bespoke Range Rovers (always based on 4.6-litre models) would not actually be made until the following year, but the announcement did lend interest to the start of the 1997 model-year. (*See* Chapter 6 for the Autobiography programme.)

The 1997 UK Limited Editions

HSE+ (1997)

The HSE+ was announced on 22 July 1997 for 1 August availability. Costing £53,000, this was a limited edition of 100 vehicles, based on the 4.6 HSE.

The HSE+ had British Racing Green metallic paint, which was extended to the sills, door mirror bodies and front apron spoiler (although the bib spoiler remained black). This colour was drawn from the Autobiography palette, although it was also offered on 1997 and 1998 models for North America, and was a standard showroom option for Rover cars. It was complemented by a cream coachline, and Mondial 18in alloy wheels from the mainstream options list were standard. Upholstery was in Lightstone leather with dark green piping.

Autobiography (1997)

The Autobiography limited edition was also announced on 22 July 1997, and consisted of just thirty vehicles based on the 4.6 HSE. On the tailgate, the model badging was replaced by a gold Autobiography decal. Each example cost £63,000, which made these the most expensive Range Rovers yet.

The Autobiography edition fulfilled the promise of the 1996 Autobiography demonstrator, and featured a Philips

The HSE+ edition was introduced over the summer of 1997; the press-release picture showed it with a 1998-season registration plate.

CARiN satellite navigation system as standard. This was visible as a monitor screen in the centre of the dashboard, above the console. As satellite navigation systems were still new and exciting in 1997, these Range Rovers were sometimes known by the CARiN name rather than as Autobiography types.

Like the contemporary HSE+, the Autobiography came in British Racing Green paint with a cream coachline, but visually was distinguished by the 18in Triple Sport alloy wheels seen on the show car. A more subtle difference was that the bib spoiler below the front apron was painted in the body colour.

The Autobiography also had a more determinedly bespoke interior, with pale Parchment leather and perforated seat facings. Contrasting Lincoln Green piping and carpet over-rugs toned in with the exterior colour, and there was burr walnut wood trim on the centre console, instrument surround, gearshift and handbrake grip.

The Diesel that Might Have Been

By 1993, Land Rover was planning a new family of diesel engines that were collectively known by the code-name of Storm. The Storm engines were to be a next stage on from

---

TECHNICAL SPECIFICATIONS, 1995–1997 MODELS

Engines:
2.5-litre diesel
BMW M51 6-cylinder diesel with cast-iron block and light-alloy head
2497cc (80 × 82.8mm)
Single overhead camshaft
Seven-bearing crankshaft
Indirect injection with turbocharger and intercooler

1995–1996 models
Compression ratio 22:1
134bhp at 4,400rpm
199lb/ft at 2,300rpm

1997 models
Compression ratio 22:1
136bhp at 4,400rpm
197lb/ft at 2,000rpm

4.0-litre V8
Land Rover V8-cylinder petrol with alloy block and cylinder heads
3947cc (93.98 × 71.1mm)
Single overhead camshaft
Five-bearing crankshaft
Lucas injection with GEMS electronic engine management system

Compression ratio 9.34:1
190bhp at 4,750rpm
236lb/ft at 3,000rpm

4.6-litre V8
Land Rover V8-cylinder petrol with alloy block and cylinder heads
4554cc (93.98 × 82mm)
Single overhead camshaft
Five-bearing crankshaft
Lucas injection with GEMS electronic engine management system

Compression ratio 9.34:1
225bhp at 4,750rpm
277lb/ft at 3,000rpm
Compression ratio 8.36:1 for some export territories
209bhp at 4,750rpm
264lb/ft at 3,000rpm

Primary gearbox:
Manual (2.5 diesel)
Five-speed, type R380
Ratios 3.69:1, 2.13:1, 1.40:1, 1.00:1, 0.73:1, reverse 3.53:1

Manual (4.0 petrol)
Five-speed R380 manual
Ratios 3.32:1, 2.13:1, 1.40:1, 1.00:1, 0.73:1, reverse 3.53:1

Automatic (2.5 diesel and 4.0 petrol)
Four-speed, ZF 4HP22
Ratios 2.48:1, 1.48:1, 1.00:1, 0.73:1, reverse 2.09:1

the Rover Group's L-series 4-cylinder diesel, which would be seen in Rover cars from 1994, and then in the Land Rover Freelander from 1997.

The Storm design was to be a modular one, and three basic derivatives were planned. These were a 2.0-litre 4-cylinder (for a future small Land Rover), a 2.5-litre 5-cylinder (for the Defender and the Discovery) and a 3.0-litre 6-cylinder (for the Range Rover). If things had gone according to plan, the Range Rover might have had a new 6-cylinder Land Rover diesel engine by the end of the 1990s.

However, BMW's purchase of the Rover Group at the start of 1994 put an end to that. The German company already had world-class 4-cylinder and 6-cylinder diesel engines in production or in preparation, and it would make no business sense for Land Rover to spend money on developing similar engines of its own. So BMW terminated development of the 4-cylinder and 6-cylinder Storm engines, but allowed Land Rover to continue work on the 5-cylinder because their own 6-cylinder was too long for the engine bay of the Discovery. A few 4-cylinder Storm engines had actually been built, but the 6-cylinder Range Rover engine probably never was. When the 5-cylinder was released in 1998, it took the name of Td5, and became the power unit for both Defender and Discovery models.

Automatic (4.6 petrol)
Four-speed, ZF 4HP24 automatic
Ratios 2.48:1, 1.48:1, 1.00:1, 0.73:1, reverse 2.09:1

Transfer gearbox:
Two-speed Borg Warner type 13-61
Ratios 1.22:1 (high) and 3.27:1 (low)

All transfer gearboxes with a self-locking viscous-coupled centre differential

Axle ratio:
3.54:1

Suspension:
Front and rear live axles with electronically controlled air springs and telescopic dampers; front axle located by cranked radius arms and Panhard rod, with anti-rollbar; rear axle located by composite trailing links and Panhard rod

Steering:
Recirculating ball system with power assistance as standard

Brakes:
Four-wheel disc brakes with dual hydraulic line, vacuum servo assistance and four-channel ABS; reverse-ventilated front discs with 11.7in diameter and four-piston calipers; solid rear discs with 12in diameter and two-piston calipers; separate internal expanding drum-type parking brake, operating on transmission output shaft

Dimensions:

Overall length:	185.6in (4,713mm)
Overall width:	74.4in (1,889mm)
Overall height:	71.6in (1,817mm) at standard ride height
Wheelbase:	108.1in (2,745mm)
Track, front:	60.6in (1,540mm)
Track, rear:	60.2in (1,530mm)

Wheels and tyres:
Various styles of five-bolt alloy wheel with 16in diameter and 7in or 8in rim; or with 18in diameter and 8in rim. Tyres with 235 or 255 section.

Kerb weight (for typical UK-market models):
4,662lb (2,115kg) – diesel manual
4,695lb (2,130kg) – diesel automatic
4,607lb (2,090kg) – 4.0 V8 manual
4,630lb (2,100kg) – 4.0 V8 automatic
4,894lb (2,220kg) – 4.6 V8

Performance:

Max. speed:	105mph (170 km/h) – diesel manual
	101mph (162km/h) – diesel automatic
	118mph (190km/h) – 4.0 V8 manual
	116mph (187km/h) – 4.0 V8 automatic
	125mph (200km/h) – 4.6 V8
0–60mph:	13.3sec – diesel manual
	14.7sec – diesel automatic
	9.9sec – 4.0 V8 manual
	10.4sec – 4.0 V8 automatic
	9.3sec – 4.6 V8

PAINT AND TRIM COMBINATIONS, 1995–1997 MODELS

Three types of paint were used on Range Rovers in this period. These were 'solid' paints (traditional standard types), 'metallic' paints (which incorporated tiny metal flakes to reflect light and give a higher sheen) and 'micatallic' paints (which incorporated tiny particles of mica to achieve a high sheen). All the metallic and micatallic paints used on Range Rovers had a clear protective coat applied over the colour coats, and these paints were known as 'clear-over-base' types. In addition, Beluga Black (a 'solid' colour) had a clear protective top coat.

Cloth upholstery was used for base models, and leather on the more expensive variants.

1995 Model-Year (September 1994 to June 1995)

For the 1995 model-year there were initially fourteen exterior paint colours. Six were carried over from the first-generation Range Rover: Alpine White, Arles Blue, Aspen Silver, Beluga Black, Portofino Red and Roman Bronze. Some of the new colours appeared in sales and service literature with abbreviated names, for example Avalon instead of Avalon Blue, and Sahara instead of Sahara Gold.

There were just two upholstery colours: Granite Grey and Saddle Brown. Granite was available with all paint colours except Roman Bronze and Sahara Gold. Saddle was available with all colours except Arles Blue, Avalon Blue, Caprice Green and Niagara Grey.

The Full List of 1995 Colours

Alpine White	Biarritz Blue	Niagara Grey
Arles Blue	Caprice Green	Portofino Red
Aspen Silver	Coniston Green	Roman Bronze
Avalon Blue	Epsom Green	Sahara Gold
Beluga Black	Montpellier Red	

1996 Model-Year (June 1995 to October 1996)

For the 1996 model-year there were again fourteen exterior paint colours, but Altai Silver, Rioja Red and Willow Green had replaced Aspen Silver, Montpellier Red and Roman Bronze. Of the 1996 colour range, one was a clear-over-base solid colour, three were metallics, four were ordinary solid colours and six were micatallics.

There were two additional upholstery colours, making the total up to four. Granite Grey and Saddle Brown remained, while Ash Grey was available in both cloth and leather and Lightstone Beige came only in leather with Ash Grey piping and Dark Stone beige carpets. Every exterior colour was now available to order with every interior colour.

The Full List of 1996 Colours

Alpine White	Biarritz Blue	Portofino Red
Altai Silver	Caprice Green	Rioja Red
Arles Blue	Coniston Green	Sahara Gold
Avalon Blue	Epsom Green	Willow Green
Beluga Black	Niagara Grey	

1997 Model-Year (October 1996 to September 1997)

Three exterior colours were replaced for the 1997 model-year. The new ones were Charleston Green, Oxford Blue and Riviera Blue, which replaced Biarritz Blue, Caprice and Sahara Gold. As before, there were fourteen colours, of which five were solids, three were metallics and six were micatallics.

The four upholstery options remained unchanged, and all types and colours were available with all exterior colours.

The Full List of 1997 Colours

Alpine White	Charleston Green	Portofino Red
Altai Silver	Coniston Green	Rioja Red
Arles Blue	Epsom Green	Riviera Blue
Avalon Blue	Niagara Grey	Willow Green
Beluga Black	Oxford Blue	

WHEEL STYLES, 1995–1997 MODELS

1995–1996 Model-Years

There were three styles of wheel for the first two model-years. These were:

Classic	Three-spoke	7×16
DBL	Five-hole	7×16
Stratos	Five-spoke	8×16

1997 Model-Year

The Classic, DBL and Stratos wheels remained available, but two new 18in wheel styles also became available from late 1996. The Mondial was available as a line-fit option, but the Triple Sport was always an accessory wheel.

Mondial	Five-spoke	8×18
Triple Sport	Three split spokes	8×18

Classic three-spoke alloy wheel.

Mondial five-spoke 18in wheel.

DBL five-hole alloy wheel.

Triple Sport accessory-fit wheel.

Stratos five-spoke alloy wheel.

CHAPTER THREE

A CHANGE OF PLAN

While a core team of designers and engineers dealt with the annual model updates that followed the launch of the 38A in 1994, a second team was assembled to look further ahead and to begin planning for the model's mid-life facelift.

Land Rover had designed the 38A to be competitive for ten years, according to John Hall in a 1995 interview with the author. Of course, this could only ever be a projection, because nobody knew for certain when other companies might produce rival products or how good those might be. Nevertheless, the 1999 model-year was identified as the time when a mid-life facelift would be necessary. As the 1999 models would be introduced towards the end of 1998, this would actually be four years into the product cycle, therefore slightly before the five-year milepost that would mark the middle of the 38A's potential production run.

All this would have been anticipated since before the 1994 launch, but by the time it came to be put into practice, BMW's purchase of Land Rover had put a new angle on things. The German company had, of course, taken a close look at Land Rover's product portfolio and at its future product plans, and had reached their own conclusions about how the Range Rover should develop.

Both BMW Chairman Bernd Pischetsrieder and its engineering chief Wolfgang Reitzle (who oversaw the transitional first year of BMW ownership) had their own views on the 38A. Reitzle in particular disliked certain features, among them the arrangement of the electric window switches on the leading edge of the centre cubby box. He is said to have considered the interior finish a special disappointment, and in their book *End of the Road: BMW and Rover – A Brand Too*

The original intention was to use BMW engines for the 1999 models. This is one of the V8s being tried out in an engine-bay mock-up...

... and here is a
BMW V8 in a running
prototype. **Note how**
the positions of several
engine ancillaries have
changed from the
mock-up.

Far (Prentice Hall, 2001), Chris Brady and Andrew Lorenz tell the following story:

> ...*on his first visit to Land Rover after the BMW acquisition, Reitzle had climbed into the new vehicle, donned an aircraft eye mask and spent five minutes touching every inch of the cabin. He then got out and wrote a list of 70 features that he believed should be changed.*

So it was no surprise that when work began on the 1999 model-year facelift, there was some serious input from BMW. Not only would there have to be improvements to the interior: understandably proud of the world-renowned engines it already had in production, BMW wanted to use these as the power plants for the 1999 Range Rover. Their own 6-cylinder diesel was already in place and should remain so, but the two Land Rover petrol V8s were old technology, and BMW wanted to replace them with their own V8 engines.

In the BMW scheme of things, the V8 engines it would have in production by the start of the Range Rover's 1999 model-year would be the M62 types, developed from the earlier M60 engines and now being prepared for 1996 introduction with swept volumes of 3.5 litres and 4.4 litres. With

a projected 235bhp and 286bhp respectively, these engines would offer the Range Rover some very real performance advantages, at the same time as they brought BMW some very real cost savings: it would, of course, be cheaper to build increased numbers of these engines at BMW's engine plant in Steyr, Austria, than to maintain a completely separate assembly line in Britain for the 4.0-litre and 4.6-litre Rover V8s.

The 3.5-litre BMW V8 was certainly considered for a time, but seems to have been dropped from the plan quite early on. The 4.4-litre, however, was installed in one or more engineering 'mules'; the likelihood is that one was built by BMW in Germany and another by Land Rover in Britain. Pictures suggest that the engine was a tight but comfortable fit within the 38A's engine bay.

However, BMW's ambitions did not stop here. Wolfgang Reitzle was determined to push the Range Rover as far up-market as he possibly could, and stories began to leak out from Land Rover that he was aiming for a flagship £100,000 Range Rover. At a time when the top models cost less than half that much, this was quite radical thinking, but in the financial climate of the mid-1990s it did not seem unrealistic. It was also a very clear indication of what a hot property BMW believed they had bought in the Range Rover.

A Range Rover with that sort of price tag was going to need more than some extra equipment to distinguish it from the ordinary models. So Reitzle decided that it should be given the ultimate in performance and refinement by using BMW's V12 engine. The latest versions of this had a swept volume of 5.4 litres (5379cc) and delivered a silky 320bhp and a massive 360lb/ft of torque. Not for nothing was this engine the one chosen to power the Rolls-Royce Silver Seraph from 1998 and, in further developed 600bhp form, the McLaren F1 supercar.

It must have been some time in 1995 when Reitzle had a pair of these engines shoehorned into Range Rovers. And shoehorned they were: among other things, there were problems with clearance between the front axle and the engine sump, and the V12 engine was so long that it barely fitted into the existing engine bay at all. The two V12 prototype vehicles were probably both converted in Germany, and seem to have remained there; Reitzle used one himself for a time, and the other one supposedly went to Pischetsrieder. Unsurprisingly, the motoring press got to hear about them, and so the news spread that a V12 Range Rover was being planned. Neither Land Rover nor BMW ever issued an official comment, of course.

Meanwhile, the 1999-model Range Rovers were being

THE V12 PROTOTYPES

Many interesting prototypes are scrapped after their development life is over, but the two V12-engined Range Rovers appear to have been fully functional vehicles that were capable of everyday use – even if some features would have been redesigned for production.

It appears that BMW eventually sold both of them to the Bahrain Royal Family. Although they were built in 1996, they were given 1999-model VINs before sale: SALLPAMC4XA-414696 and SALLPAMC4XA-419123. The C in the eighth position clearly indicates the V12 engine, the 4 shows that both were LHD automatics, and the X is the 1999 designator (see Appendix A). Land Rover has no official record of either vehicle in its Traceability Department.

The **BMW V12 engine** was a very tight squeeze in the Range Rover's engine bay, but here it is in a prototype. The slightly untidy engine bay suggests that the vehicle was still under construction when this picture was taken.

By late 1995, the design studio was working on options for the planned 1999 models; Mike Sampson drew up this one for the lengthened front end in October 1995.

Another Mike Sampson proposal, dating from January 1996.

The intention was to modify the rear end as well, and this was Mike Sampson's January 1996 proposal.

'Essentially, we had to change the front and rear ends,' he remembered in 2003. 'We were also looking at some interior changes.' Sketches from the period show various proposals to make the vehicle look wider from the rear by repositioning the lights and increasing the horizontal emphasis, and to give greater definition to the front end.

However, the biggest problem was the need to fit that V12 engine under the Range Rover's bonnet. There simply was not enough room, and Mike Sampson remembered that the engineering installation demanded a front overhang increased by a massive 160mm (6.3in). Trying to disguise that, and also to keep the approach angle acceptable, proved very difficult indeed.

A full-size styling model of the proposed 1999 Range Rover was made for Land Rover by an outside company, and BMW made their own model separately. But that was as far as it went. Over the summer of 1996, a Lifetime Planning exercise reviewed plans for the 38A's future, and BMW decided that the cost of the proposed 1999 model-year changes was unreasonably high. Far better, the review concluded, to put the money into a new third-generation Range Rover and to launch this earlier than originally anticipated. It would bring a freshness to the Range Rover that could not be achieved through the planned facelift, and it would help the model to keep a step ahead of its rivals.

So the 1999 model-year facelift was formally cancelled in September 1996, and the focus of major development work switched to the third-generation Range Rover or L30. The aim was to have this ready by the end of 2001, and to launch

planned with a number of cosmetic changes as well as the new engines. George Thomson, who had led the original 38A styling team, would have loved to have got involved with this, 'to eradicate some of the earlier criticisms of the vehicle', as he put it. However, after the 1994 launch he had remained on the main 38A team and had responsibility for incremental model-year styling updates, which meant he was too busy. So Mike Sampson, another key member of the original styling team, was put in charge of the styling changes for the 1999 models.

The proposed 1999 model-year got as far as this full-size styling mock-up, incorporating one of Mike Sampson's front-end proposals.

The rear of the full-size styling car (bizarrely badged as a 2.5 DSE) shows two alternative proposals.

it as a 2002 model. And that was exactly what happened, although in the meantime BMW had sold Land Rover to Ford, who changed its development code name to L322.

The decision to abandon the comprehensive 1999 model-year makeover led to some quite radical changes in the 38A forward model programme. By the time the BMW engines and associated 1999 model-year changes were cancelled, the 1997 model Range Rovers were already in production. So the earliest effect of the decision was on the 1998 model Range Rovers. These were now seen as the first building block on the way to the launch of L30 in 2001. So although they would have relatively few new features, they would be accompanied by marketing activity that was intended to generate additional press and customer interest and also enhance the aspirational nature of the Range Rover.

As for the 1999 model-year, that was still seen as the turning point in the 38A's production life, when more major changes would be necessary. So a major programme of interior improvements was set in train (partly at least to deal with the criticisms Reitzle had made earlier), and Land Rover's engine team was given the job of overhauling the existing V8 engines and making them more suited to customer demands. Other changes were aimed to make the Range Rover a still more credible contender for luxury car sales, moving it ever closer to what BMW had in mind for the third-generation model. Even so, the news that a V12 engine had been in the pipeline did not go away, and the news that it had been cancelled did not leak out to the public. As a result, there were many disappointed faces outside Land Rover when the 1999 models appeared without it.

The extra length of the nose is barely discernible in this side view of the styling model.

THE 1998 MODELS

By the time of the 1998 model-year, the Range Rover was in a strong position. During the 1997 calendar year (so, to a quarter of the way through the 1998 model-year), it had just under a quarter of the UK luxury car market, coming second to the Jaguar XJ range. It was the best seller in the French luxury market, although the going was harder in Germany, where it claimed only about 5 per cent (around 2,000 vehicles a year) of the luxury market against domestic stalwarts Mercedes-Benz and BMW. Even so, Germany was the second-largest market for the Range Rover in Europe. It was the luxury market sector leader in Italy and Spain, and in Japan it had claimed a 10 per cent share of the luxury import segment. In the USA, it accounted for 1.3 per cent of the total luxury car market.

Land Rover treated the 1998 model-year as a holding operation for the Range Rover. An internal marketing document read:

> Besides the general goal of quality improvement, for business reasons this model year has been developed with minimal investment. Most changes have been made to comply with forthcoming legislation; however, the features included were identified to offer some visual change for little investment, thereby appearing to offer better value for money.

So when volume production of the 1998 models began on 7 July 1997, the visual exterior changes were mainly to paint and wheels. There were six new colours among the fourteen on offer, and all paints were now water-based; all solid colours now became clear-over-base types, with a lacquer top coat that gave an extra lustre. All wheels were given 'jewelled' centre caps with the Land Rover logo in colour. The 1998 models also came with five matching alloy wheels instead of four alloys and a steel spare, a combination that customers had not liked.

The wheel choices also changed, and overall offered a much more attractive selection than before. Entry-level models came with new Futura 16×7 wheels, while the mid-range SE and DSE types switched to new Pursuit wheels with the same dimensions. Both had 235×16 tyres. The HSE retained its 16×8 Stratos five-spoke wheels with 255×16 tyres, but could again have Mondial 18×8 alloys with 255×18 tyres as a line-fit option. Triple Sport 18×8 alloys remained available as a Land Rover Parts accessory, and a new 16×8

design called Spyder was made available for use as required on limited editions.

Minor changes affected the front end, too. Although the HSE was unchanged, the entry-level models now gained the lower bib spoiler standard on the higher-specification models, and the SE petrol and DSE manual diesel models gained the fog lights that had been exclusive to the HSE. This change was not replicated on the DSE automatic models, though, because the transmission oil cooler occupied part of the space they needed. Then at the rear, the third stop lamp that was already standard for some countries became a standard fitment for all Range Rovers, so meeting new United Nations legislation (UN Regulation 48) that was to be adopted in Europe in 1998.

The 1998-season passenger cabin changes were more obvious to most people who came into contact with one of the new models. On all seats, a six-pleat design replaced the existing three-panel styles, and all leather seats now came with Ash Grey piping, as did their head rests. Land Rover's view was that the result looked more traditionally British. Meanwhile, a more sophisticated fabric called Langdale cloth replaced the early 'towelling' type, and cloth seats lost their piping. This new cloth had a hint of a contrasting colour running throughout, and was accompanied by Lichen cloth on the sides of the seats.

Twin airbags also became standard on all Range Rovers for 1998, eliminating an early anomaly. Leather gearshift grips became standard on all derivatives, and the walnut door-trim inserts that had earlier distinguished the HSE (TL3) models now became standard on the SE (TL2) models as well. Standard on all 1998 models was a new radio aerial amplifier that gave better reception, and the ICE systems were also upgraded. Entry-level models now had the eight-speaker Clarion system that had been on 1997's SE models; the SE models now had ten speakers; and the HSE took on a new and very effective eleven-speaker harmon/kardon system with remote controls on the steering wheel.

Some of these changes helped to distance the Range Rover from its new stablemate, the Discovery Series II, that was also announced in autumn 1998. In fact, one Range Rover change for 1998 had initially been developed for that new model and was then adapted to suit the flagship range. This was the so-called 'fast throttle', which provided a potentiometer to convey accelerator demands to the engine control unit instead of using a cable. All it really did, as Land Rover admitted in internal documents, was to give the impression of improving acceleration because of reduced

This 1998 Range Rover was converted to a camera car for use by Land Rover's own photographic team. By the time this picture was taken, it had been updated with later specification lights.

pedal movement; actual acceleration remained unchanged. In low range, the 'fast throttle' was disengaged, so giving the longer pedal travel necessary for fine control of speed when driving off-road.

The 1998 Special Models

Against this background of minimum change, the 1998 model-year in Britain was given additional impetus as it began in November 1997 with a special edition called the DSE+, which had been carefully specified to represent good value for money. At about the same time, the French and Belgian National Sales Companies collaborated on a special edition called the Holland & Holland, and there was a Range Rover DeLuxe special edition in Germany as well.

Company documents refer to plans for a 'halo' edition in 1998, which would showcase several of the Autobiography options. This probably materialized as the Range Rover Vogue 50, which was announced to coincide with Land Rover's fiftieth anniversary in April but did not actually go on sale until June. There was a quite different 50th Anniversary Edition in the USA at about the same time (*see* Chapter 5), while Japan had a special edition of its own (*see* below). British buyers were offered yet another limited edition in June, this one called the dHSE and specifically intended to test customer reception of a model that combined the top HSE trim level with the diesel engine. There were then two more special editions for Britain in August 1998, called the County and the Vogue SE, adding features to the entry-level and top-model Range Rovers respectively.

The four British limited editions – the Vogue 50, dHSE, County and the Vogue SE – were all what Land Rover called '98.5 model-year' types. That designation applied to all Range Rovers built after 1 June with minor changes to meet new European legislation, known as ECD2 (and more familiarly as 'Euro 2'). The changes were to catalytic converters, to the electronic EGR systems, and to anti-theft provisions, and all new vehicles had to comply by the time the legislation became effective on 1 October.

The 1998 UK Limited Editions

DSE+ (November 1997)

There were 400 examples of the DSE+, which was intended to represent good value for money by offering a collection of special features as standard at a considerable saving over buying them individually. The automatic-only DSE+ was priced at £45,995, or £3,500 more than a standard DSE automatic.

The DSE+ was available in four colours – Epsom Green, Rioja Red, Oxford Blue and White Gold. All had a single coachline, which was grey on White Gold models but cream with the other three colours. The front apron and bumpers were painted to match the bodywork (although the bib spoiler was not painted), as were the sills and door-mirror bodies. The wheels were the special 'limited edition' new Spyder 16in alloys, and the tailgate badging was deleted.

Seats were upholstered in Lightstone leather, with contrasting piping – Tapestry Red with Rioja Red coachwork, Atlantis Blue with Oxford Blue, or Lincoln Green with Epsom Green and White Gold. The standard SE specification was boosted by the latest harman/kardon eleven-speaker in-car entertainment system with CD autochanger and steering-wheel remote controls, plus an electric sunroof and electrically adjustable front seats.

Vogue 50 (June 1998)

Land Rover celebrated its fiftieth anniversary in 1998 with a series of 'Collector's Edition' vehicles based on all four model ranges. The Range Rover-based model was derived from the 4.6 HSE and was called the Vogue 50.

The original plan was to build just fifty examples, of which thirty were to have a CARiN satellite navigation system and were to be priced at £71,000, while the remaining twenty were to come without the satnav and were to cost £68,000. Even at these prices – the highest yet for a non-bespoke Range Rover in the UK – demand was such that Special Vehicles had to increase the production run to fifty-five examples.

Every Range Rover Vogue 50 was painted in Atlantis Blue, a micatallic paint created for the Collector's Edition range of vehicles. The sills, bumpers, apron spoiler and mirror heads were all in the body colour, and there was a single White Gold coachline. The wheels were 18in Proline alloys (a new design at that stage), the tailgate carried a special 'Vogue 50' badge, and there was darkened privacy glass all round. A numbered '50th Anniversary' brass plate was fitted to the front face of each B-post.

Seats had Parchment 'full' leather (that is, the sides and backs were in leather as well as the facings), with Atlantis Blue piping. The gearshift, handbrake cover and door pulls were also in Atlantis Blue, and there were Atlantis Blue over-rugs. Chromed interior door handles helped to set off a deluxe walnut wood trim set and matching fold-down picnic tables on the backs of the front seats. A video player fed twin television screens mounted in the rear of the front seat headrests, and there was a three-piece set of 'Vogue 50' branded travel luggage made of black Nappa leather.

In this period the **LRSV** role in creating special Range Rovers became much more prominent.
This is the 1998 Vogue 50 edition, with the then new 18in Proline alloy wheels.

LEFT: **Although the Autobiography programme was capable of turning out some extremely eye-catching Range Rovers, the Vogue 50 was deliberately discreet. Even the special Atlantis Blue paint, which could 'flip' to green in certain lights, seems quite subdued here.** NICK DIMBLEBY

BOTTOM LEFT: **There was, of course, a discreet special edition badge on the tailgate.** NICK DIMBLEBY

BOTTOM RIGHT: **For 1998, the Vogue 50's light-coloured Parchment leather and additional wood were the height of luxury – and distinctively different from what was available on mainstream models.** NICK DIMBLEBY

The 1998 dHSE special edition combined the diesel engine with HSE equipment levels. The grille on the left of the front apron identified it as a diesel automatic – and of course it couldn't have the fog lights of the 4.6 HSE.

dHSE (June 1998)

With 600 examples, the dHSE became the largest UK limited edition of the second-generation Range Rover. Its success justified Land Rover's intention of making a diesel HSE a standard showroom model, which happened in October 1999. At £47,075, the dHSE cost £3,400 less than a 4.6 HSE.

The dHSE came in six colours – Cobar Blue, Epsom Green, Niagara Grey, Oxford Blue, Rioja Red and White Gold. Bumpers, sills and mirror heads were painted in the body colour, and all colours except White Gold had a single cream coachline; with White Gold the coachline was in grey. The wheels were 16in Stratos alloys with their standard 255-section tyres.

The base model was an automatic DSE, to which were added an electric sunroof, rear-axle ETC, the harmon/kardon ICE system, electric front seats (without a memory function), an auto-dimming rear-view mirror, and cup holders in the underside of the reversible cubby box lid. All examples had Lightstone leather upholstery with contrasting piping. The piping was in Atlantis Blue with Cobar Blue and Oxford Blue paint, in Lincoln Green with Epsom Green and White Gold, or in Tapestry Red with Niagara Grey and Rioja Red.

Interestingly, the dHSE did not have the mud flaps standard on the 4.6 HSE, and did not have the fog lamps – which could not be fitted because of the position of the oil cooler behind the front apron.

County (August 1998)

The Range Rover County was based on an entry-level 4.0-litre V8 with standard automatic gearbox, but its £41,995 on-the-road price was intended to tempt buyers at this end of the market to spend a little more. The County name was familiar from other Land Rover models, but had not been used on a UK-market Range Rover before.

The 240 examples of this limited edition came in Epsom Green, Niagara Grey, Oxford Blue or White Gold. The mirror heads and part of the front apron spoiler were painted to match the body, and there was a twin coachline on each side. Model badging was deleted from the tailgate, but there were no County badges anywhere on the vehicles. Wheels were the 16in Spyder design then reserved for special editions.

Every Range Rover County had seats upholstered in Lightstone leather with matching piping, door pulls, handbrake grip and gearshift knob. The steering wheel was trimmed in duo-tone leather, and there were chrome interior door-release handles. Other interior hardware was in Ash Grey (with Niagara Grey and Oxford Blue paintwork) or Saddle (with Epsom Green and White Gold).

Vogue SE (August 1998)

The Vogue SE was based on the outgoing 1998-model 4.6 HSE, and there were 220 examples in four paint colours. The on-the-road price was £54,495.

The four colour options were Epsom Green, Oxford Blue, Rioja Red and White Gold, and the sills, bumpers, front apron and mirror heads were all body-coloured. Every vehicle had a twin coachline in gold, except with White Gold, when it was in dark green. There was no model derivative badge on the tailgate, and no Vogue SE identification anywhere on the vehicle. The wheels were the latest 18in Proline alloys, as previewed on the Vogue 50 a few months earlier.

Upholstery was in Lightstone leather, piped in green with Epsom Green and White Gold paint, in Atlantis Blue with Oxford Blue, or in Tapestry Red with Rioja Red. The gearshift knob and handbrake grip were also trimmed with the contrasting colour used on the piping. There was additional wood trim on the console switch panel, and around the HEVAC controls, ICE and instrument pack.

The 1998 European and Japanese Limited Editions

Holland & Holland (February 1997, Belgium and France)

It was probably the French National Sales Company, which had a strong track record in creating its own limited editions, that initiated this one. The alliance with luxury gunmaker Holland & Holland preceded Land Rover's own more formal

arrangement by some two years, and these limited-edition Range Rovers were sold in both France and Belgium. They were promoted on their 'Britishness', and the press launch was held at Holland & Holland's shooting grounds in West Wycombe in February 1997.

These limited-edition models were produced locally by modifying standard vehicles, and were not a product of Land Rover Special Vehicles at Solihull. The base vehicle was a 2.5 DSE or 4.0 SE, in either Epsom Green or Willow Green. Features were Stratos wheels from the HSE, a Lightstone interior with a special Holland & Holland dashboard plaque, Holland & Holland decal logos on the rear wings and tailgate, a CD player, and a collection of special luggage. At launch in 1997, the French price was 349,000FF with either engine, when the standard SE and DSE each cost 337,000FF.

DeLuxe (late 1997 or early 1998, Germany)

The Range Rover DeLuxe was a seventy-five strong special edition built by LRSV and probably based on the 4.6 HSE. All examples had Oxford Blue paint with Autobiography-style two-tone leather seats; the basic seat colour was Ash Grey, while the centre panels and piping were in Granite. There was a 'de luxe' wood dashboard, matched by burr walnut picnic tables on the seat backs. A CARiN satnav system was standard, together with a TV and video system for rear-seat passengers.

The Holland & Holland edition for France and Belgium is seen here as a 4.0 SE model. Note the HSE-style wheels and the special decal on the rear wing.
NICK DIMBLEBY

Other special features were body-colour bumpers and mirror bodies, chrome interior door handles, and leather-trimmed door pulls, glove box and knee bolster. Each vehicle was also fitted with a plaque that was engraved with the name of its first owner.

The German custom specialist Arden, based at Krefeld, supposedly had some involvement with the DeLuxe edition, but it is not clear what that was.

Unnamed Edition (late 1997 or early 1998, Japan)

There was an LRSV-built limited edition for Japan, about which few details are available. It was essentially a 4.6 HSE in British Racing Green paint from the Autobiography colour palette. The bumpers, sills and mirror heads were painted in the body colour.

The interior had two-tone seats from the Autobiography options list, with Lightstone as the main colour complemented by green centre panels and piping. There were leather-trimmed door pulls, glove box and knee bolster, and the dashboard had a deluxe wood finish, which was probably burr walnut.

50th Anniversary (1998, Japan)

Land Rover's Japanese national sales company created its own 50th Anniversary edition by adding a few special features to standard models. Few details are available, but it is clear that there was a tailgate decal reading 'Anniversary 1948–1998'; special floor mats in brown, with a UK-style '50th Anniversary Edition' tag, also seem to have been in the specification.

THE 1999 MODELS

Even though the original plan for the 1999 model-year had been more elaborate, this model-year was still seen as the point when the model would need its mid-life facelift. So Land Rover refreshed it with revised petrol engines, multiple interior improvements and another collection of new wheel designs. Less obvious but perhaps equally important was additional safety from side airbags and the extension of ETC to all four wheels. To withstand the additional strains that this would impose, a four-pin differential became standard in the front axle, matching that already used at the rear.

The Japanese 50th Anniversary edition had a unique tailgate decal that read 'Anniversary, 1948–1998'.

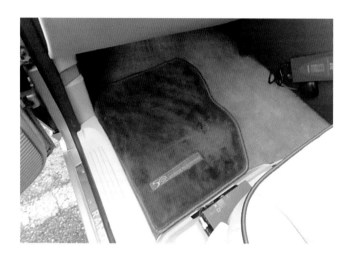

There were special floor mats, too, with the same green tag as on the UK 50th Anniversary vehicles, but with a different background colour.

The Range Rover had done well during the 1998 model-year, maintaining its sales volume in spite of increased competition. That new competition was primarily from Mercedes-Benz (whose single-model ML range would soon be broadened to present a challenge that straddled both the Discovery and Range Rover line-ups), but in the USA there was also the Lexus LX470, which was a luxury derivative of the Toyota Land Cruiser.

There had been significant Range Rover quality improvements during the 1998 model-year, which had helped re-establish customer confidence. The task of the 1999 models was now to position the Range Rover even further up-market, and to continue preparing the way for the launch of its L30 replacement in 2001. But a marketing document of the time shows that Land Rover recognized the limitations of the product they were selling: 'Range Rover cannot compete with traditional luxury vehicles on their terms,' it read. 'To succeed it must be positioned as "peerless", eg the unrivalled alternative to the luxury car.' So the physical changes to the Range Rover for 1999 were accompanied by some major efforts from the marketing team to persuade potential buyers to see the vehicle as somehow apart from the mainstream of luxury cars and thus without any direct competition.

Everything was in place by mid-April 1998, and build of the QP (Quality Proving) batch of 1999 Range Rovers began on 17 April; these followed by the M (Methods) build vehicles on 18 June; and then volume production began on 1 September. That was also the date on which the press launch of the new models began, the dealers having had their introduction at an event beginning on 26 August. The public introduction of the new models then followed at the Paris Motor Show during September.

There were surprisingly few exterior changes for the 1999 Range Rovers, and that may be one reason why the new-model press launch held in Surrey at the start of September 1998 included several Autobiography models; they were more different to look at than the standard models. There were just a couple of changes to the colour palette, as Java Black replaced Beluga Black, and Blenheim Silver replaced Altai Silver, but the most obvious changes were to the wheels yet again.

For most countries, entry-level Range Rovers now came with the Pursuit alloys that had been standard on the 1998 mid-range models. The SE and DSE took on the Spyder alloys with 255-section tyres that had been reserved for limited editions in 1998, and the HSE models came with new Lightning wheels and 255-section tyres. All these standard wheel types had a 16in diameter, but there were three 18in designs available as well, all running on 255-section tyres. The existing Mondial line-fit and Triple Sport accessory-fit options were joined by a new ten-spoke design called Hurricane. Then for limited-edition use only, the 1999 choice was a 16in alloy wheel called Typhoon and running on 255-section tyres. The major exception to all this was the USA, which took its own selection of wheel designs, as explained in Chapter 5.

Pictured at Land Rover's spiritual home of Eastnor Castle, this 1999 model has the new Lightning five-spoke alloy wheels.

WHEEL STYLES, 1998–1999 MODELS

The 1998 Model-Year

The Stratos, Mondial and Triple Sport styles remained available, but all of them now had 'jewelled' centre caps. There were two new 'standard' wheel styles, which replaced the Classic and DBL types. They were:

Futura	Three-spoke	7×16
Pursuit	Five-spoke	7×16

Futura alloy wheel.

Pursuit alloy wheel.

The 1999 Model-Year

The Pursuit and Spyder wheels now became the entry-level and SE fits, and a new design called Lightning was introduced for the HSE. The optional Mondial remained available, and was joined by a new 18in option called Hurricane. The new Typhoon style was reserved for special editions, and the Triple Sport remained available as an accessory wheel.

In addition, two new styles were used on some limited editions:

Spyder	Five-spoke	8×16
Proline	Five-spoke	8×18

Spyder alloy wheel.

The 18in Proline wheel was introduced on some late 1998 model special editions, and later became available for the Discovery Series II under the name of 'Pro Sport'.

The new wheels for 1999 were:

Typhoon	Five-spoke	7×16
Lightning	Five-spoke	8×16
Hurricane	Five split spokes	8×18

Typhoon alloy wheel.

Lightning alloy wheel.

Hurricane 18in wheel.

A really major effort had gone into improving the interior ambience, because that was where buyers would notice it most. The brief to the Land Rover stylists had been to improve the look and feel of the passenger cabin, and so the changes affected mainly those elements that were regularly looked at or touched by the Range Rover's occupants.

Although the cloth seats were unchanged, changes to the leather upholstery were immediately obvious, because the pleating was now extended to cover the top as well as the lower backrest panels. Saddle stitching was added to make it more obvious that this was leather, and panelled map pockets were now added to the seat backs. A new brown colour called Walnut replaced the earlier Saddle option, which had come in for some customer criticism. Electric height adjustment for the driver's seat was made standard across the whole range, and every seat with electric adjustment (which

The **CARiN** satellite navigation option, pictured in a 1999 Range Rover. NICK DIMBLEBY

A small cloth tag on each front seat advertised the presence of the 'thorax' airbag on 1999 models.

of course included the passenger's seat on some models) now came with the two-position memory function.

All front seats, both cloth and leather, now incorporated 'thorax' airbags, too, to increase occupant protection in a side impact. A small cloth tag reading 'airbag' on the outer side of each seat advertised the presence of this otherwise invisible improvement. It was a change of which Land Rover was rather proud, as the only other remotely competitive vehicle to offer such a feature was the new Mercedes-Benz ML. All the 1999 models also had seat-belt pre-tensioners and load limiters, although these were invisible improvements.

The changes to the door trims were more subtle, but the chrome door handles pioneered through the Autobiography scheme were now standard on all Range Rovers. The door-

The new Thor V8 engines introduced on 1999 models were distinguished by their tubular inlet manifold – but this time there was no identification to distinguish 4.0-litre from 4.6-litre.

mounted armrests were larger, too, and on HSE models were now fully trimmed in leather with saddle stitching. On entry-level models and the mid-range SE types they were trimmed in PVC but with a cloth insert or a leather one as appropriate to the upholstery.

On the facia, there were several surface and colour changes. The main functional switches on 1999 models were all black to match the ICE and HEVAC controls, and Alpine ICE units replaced Clarion types on all models; they were nevertheless branded with the Range Rover name rather than the Alpine one. The centre console and switch panel took on a new, softer-feel covering in Ash Grey, and at long last the plastic cubby box lid was upholstered as well, with Ash Grey leather that featured saddle stitching. The console's side cheeks were colour-matched to the trim.

Even though there were no BMW V8s as originally planned, the 1999 models did have extensively revised Land Rover V8 engines. The main brief to the designers had been to improve refinement, but the development programme – called Project Thor – also embraced changes needed to meet forthcoming new emissions regulations in various countries.

For the Thor engines, the designers provided a new structural sump that was designed to improve engine rigidity. To save weight, this was made of cast alloy. The engine mounts were also redeveloped to absorb any residual vibrations before they were transmitted through the bodyshell.

Increasing bottom-end and mid-range torque was also identified as a way of improving refinement, because the engine would create less noise and vibration if it was not being worked so hard while accelerating. So a new engine-management map and a new inlet manifold enabled the new engines to deliver more torque at lower engine speeds (although there were small power losses at the top end). The new manifold had eight curved tubular intakes, which formed a distinctive visual characteristic of the 4.0-litre and 4.6-litre Thor engines.

A 4.6-litre Thor engine, pictured at the 1999 model-year media launch event.

The engine-management system was not just remapped: it was completely new. Instead of the GEMS system, the Thor engines had a German-made Bosch Motronic system, as favoured for BMW's own engines. This had a digital processor to control both fuel injection and ignition, so allowing more precise control of power and torque characteristics as well as of emissions. It also required a crank position sensor, which was mounted on the flywheel along with an engine speed sensor.

The Motronic ECU actually had two separate maps, one designed to give rapid accelerator response for road use, and the other a more graduated response suitable for the fine control needed in off-road driving. Selection of the appropriate map was automatic (and was achieved through the high–low range transfer gearbox control), and a potentiometer between accelerator and engine was used to measure power demand. Meanwhile, to ensure maximum ignition reliability and to reduce maintenance as well, the Thor engines also had twin ignition coils, one for each bank of cylinders, plus long-life double-platinum spark plugs and silicon HT leads.

With both Thor engines, the four-speed ZF automatic gearbox now became the only option. So the BMW diesel engine, itself unchanged for the 1999 model-year, was now the only one that could be ordered with a manual gearbox in the Range Rover. The change simplified production to a degree, but it was also an important step in changing perceptions of the Range Rover: to all intents and purposes, it was now an automatic-only model, as befitted a luxury-class passenger car.

There were further adjustments to the line-up later in the 1999 model-year. From February 1999, a County SE limited edition encouraged British buyers to spend an extra £1,000 on a better equipped, entry-level model. At the same time, a Vogue SE limited edition arrived, with a price just above the 4.6 HSE. The final change to the 1999 line-up then came in May, when a diesel-engined HSE, this time called the 2.5 DHSE with a capital D, arrived as a regular production model – but the model-year was not rounded off until August, when yet another Vogue SE limited edition helped to prepare the way for the higher equipment levels of the 2000 model-year.

The 1999 UK Limited Editions

County SE (February 1999)

The County SE was created to allow the Range Rover to counter new rivals in the £40,000–£45,000 price bracket. It cost £42,595 on the road, and was based on the 1998 County limited edition, but with additional features that reflected dealer feedback.

This edition was based on an entry-level diesel or 4.0-litre petrol V8 model, in either case with the automatic gearbox. To this were added 16in Spyder alloy wheels from the Trim Level 2 (SE and DSE) models, and a collection of exterior finish details and interior additions. There were 250 County SE models, equally divided between the two engine types. The V8s were built in December 1998, and the diesels followed in January 1999.

There were four colour options. Most numerous were County SEs in Oxford Blue, with ninety examples; there were sixty in Rioja Red, fifty in Blenheim Silver and fifty in Woodcote Green. There was a single coachline below the side rubbing-strip, in black with Blenheim Silver, but in silver with the other three colours. The front bumper was partly painted in the body colour, and the mirror heads were also colour-coded. There was no derivative badging on the tailgate, and there were no County SE badges anywhere on the vehicle.

These were the first limited-edition Range Rovers to have their interior trim colours selected from the standard showroom option list. There was Granite Grey leather with Ash Grey piping on vehicles painted in Oxford Blue or Woodcote Green, and Ash Grey leather with Granite piping

A BIGGER DIESEL ENGINE

During 1999, Land Rover is believed to have assembled a batch of twenty-five Range Rovers with BMW's new M57 3.0-litre diesel engine in place of the standard production 2.5-litre type. The 3.0-litre engine was planned for the L30 third-generation Range Rover, whose production was then only a couple of years in the future, and this was probably a test batch to gain experience of how the engine performed in a Range Rover.

However, none of these vehicles has ever come to light. It is likely that they were all scrapped after their test duties were over, and that none escaped from Land Rover ownership. But interesting test vehicles very often do escape into the hands of ordinary owners…

**The County SE special
edition came with
Spyder alloy wheels.
This is a V8 model.**

on County SEs in Blenheim Silver and Rioja Red. In every case, the door pulls, gearshift knob and handbrake grip were trimmed to match the piping, and the steering wheel was trimmed in duotone Granite and Ash leather.

Vogue SE (February 1999)

The Vogue SE special edition went on sale in February 1999, alongside the County limited edition. It was based on a 4.6 HSE with a number of enhancements, and cost £54,495 on the road.

There were 220 examples, with four colour options:

**The third version of the Vogue SE in August
1999 had tailgate identification.**

Epsom Green, Oxford Blue, Rioja Red and White Gold. In all cases the sills, bumpers, front apron and mirror heads were painted to match the body. Every vehicle had a twin coachline in gold, except with White Gold, when it was in dark green. There was no model derivative badge on the tailgate, and no Vogue SE identification anywhere on the vehicle. The wheels were 18in Proline alloys.

Seats were upholstered in Lightstone leather, piped in green with Epsom Green and White Gold paint, in Atlantis Blue with Oxford Blue, or in Tapestry Red with Rioja Red. The gearshift knob and handbrake grip were also leather trimmed, with the contrasting colour used on the piping. There was additional wood trim on the console switch panel and around the HEVAC controls, ICE and instrument pack.

Vogue SE (August 1999)

This third Vogue SE limited edition (there had been one in 1998) was again based on the 4.6 HSE. There were 150 examples, in four different micatallic paints. Of these, fifty were in Java Black, forty in Epsom Green, and thirty each in Oxford Blue and Rioja Red.

Unlike the two earlier Vogue SE special editions, this one had 18in Hurricane wheels. The main reason appears to have been that the Proline wheels were in heavy demand for the Discovery Series II (where they were called the Pro Sport), and that supplies could not be stepped up for the limited-edition Range Rover.

The 1999 Japanese Limited Edition

In the first half of 1999, Japanese customers were offered a most unusual Autobiography edition, which was partly created at Solihull and partly in-territory. Numbers, prices and other details are unfortunately not available.

This edition was created from a kit of parts shipped out to Japan, which could be incorporated into fully built vehicles that were already in stock. It consisted of a full wood kit and interior chrome package, plus a full set of seat covers to permit a retrim, with a leather enhancement pack (for the door pulls, glove box and knee bolster) in a contrasting colour.

The 1999 German Limited Edition

Some sources claim that there was a Westminster edition for Germany in 1999, but it is not clear whether this really existed, or if there is some confusion with the 2001 Westminster edition (*see* Chapter 4).

The supposed 1999 Westminster edition appears to have been based on a 4.6-litre HSE model. It featured body-colour bumpers, sills and mirror bodies, with seats trimmed in a combination of Ash and Granite greys. The wood was Anthracite, and there were satellite navigation and TV/video options.

TECHNICAL SPECIFICATIONS, 1998–1999 MODELS

Engines:
2.5-litre diesel
BMW M51 6-cylinder diesel with cast-iron block and light-alloy head
2497cc (80 × 82.8mm)
Single overhead camshaft
Seven-bearing crankshaft
Indirect injection with turbocharger and intercooler

Compression ratio 22:1
136bhp at 4,400rpm
197lb/ft at 2,000rpm

4.0-litre V8
Land Rover V8-cylinder petrol with alloy block and cylinder heads
3947cc (93.98 × 71.1mm)
Single overhead camshaft
Five-bearing crankshaft
Lucas injection with GEMS electronic engine-management system (1998 models)
Bosch injection with Motronic 5.2.1 electronic engine-management system (1999 models)

Compression ratio 9.34:1 (1998 models)
9.38:1 (1999 models)
190bhp at 4,750rpm (1998 models)
185bhp at 4,750rpm (1999 models)
236lb/ft at 3,000rpm (1998 models)
250lb/ft at 2,600rpm (1999 models)

4.6-litre V8
Land Rover V8-cylinder petrol with alloy block and cylinder heads
4554cc (93.98 × 82mm)
Single overhead camshaft
Five-bearing crankshaft
Lucas injection with GEMS electronic engine-management system (1998 models)
Bosch injection with Motronic 5.2.1 electronic engine-management system (1999 models)

Compression ratio 9.34:1 (1998 models)
9.38:1 (1999 models)
225bhp at 4,750rpm (1998 models)
218bhp at 4,750rpm (1999 models)
277lb/ft at 3,000rpm (1998 models)
294lb/ft at 2,600rpm (1999 models)

Primary gearbox:
Manual (2.5 diesel)
Five-speed, type R380
Ratios 3.69:1, 2.13:1, 1.40:1, 1.00:1, 0.73:1, reverse 3.53:1

Manual (4.0 petrol)
Five-speed R380 manual
Ratios 3.32:1, 2.13:1, 1.40:1, 1.00:1, 0.73:1, reverse 3.53:1

Automatic (2.5 diesel and 4.0 petrol)
Four-speed, ZF 4HP22
Ratios 2.48:1, 1.48:1, 1.00:1, 0.73:1, reverse 2.09:1

WHAT THE PRESS THOUGHT

The body shape is undeniably a RR and has become more accepted than perhaps it was at launch.

This is an adept and extremely capable off-road vehicle, far more so than most owners will ever know.
(*Land Rover Monthly*, December 1998)

Comfort and refinement [in the 4.0-litre model] are close enough to the high standards Jaguar and BMW owners expect but in a genuine, practical off-roader.
(*Land Rover Monthly*, March 1999)

Nothing of this stature built around a ladder chassis could be expected to ride like a saloon, but even so, the [air suspension] system could use a little work to control the excesses of bounce and roll.
(*Top Gear*, September 1999)

Automatic (4.6 petrol)
Four-speed, ZF 4HP24 automatic
Ratios 2.48:1, 1.48:1, 1.00:1, 0.73:1, reverse 2.09:1

Transfer gearbox:
Two-speed Borg Warner type 13-61
Ratios 1.22:1 (high) and 3.27:1 (low)

All transfer gearboxes came with a self-locking viscous-coupled centre differential

Axle ratio:
3.54:1

Suspension:
Front and rear live axles with electronically controlled air springs and telescopic dampers; front axle located by cranked radius arms and Panhard rod, with anti-rollbar; rear axle located by composite trailing links and Panhard rod

Steering:
Recirculating ball system with power assistance as standard

Brakes:
Four-wheel disc brakes with dual hydraulic line, vacuum servo assistance and four-channel ABS; reverse-ventilated front discs with 11.7in diameter and four-piston calipers; solid rear discs with 12in diameter and two-piston calipers; separate internal expanding drum-type parking brake, operating on transmission output shaft

Dimensions:
Overall length: 185.6in (4,713mm)

Overall width:	74.4in (1,889mm)
Overall height:	71.6in (1,817mm) at standard ride height
Wheelbase:	108.1in (2,745mm)
Track, front:	60.6in (1,540mm)
Track, rear:	60.2in (1,530mm)

Wheels and tyres:
Various styles of five-bolt alloy wheel with 16in diameter and 7in or 8in rim; or with 18in diameter and 8in rim. Tyres with 235 or 255 section.

Kerb weight (for typical UK-market models):
4,662lb (2,115kg) – diesel manual
4,695lb (2,130kg) – diesel automatic
4,607lb (2,090kg) – 4.0 V8 manual
4,630lb (2,100kg) – 4.0 V8 automatic
4,894lb (2,220kg) – 4.6 V8

Performance:

Max. speed:	105mph (170km/h) – diesel manual
	101mph (162km/h) – diesel automatic
	118mph (190km/h) – 4.0 V8 manual
	116mph (187km/h) – 4.0 V8 automatic
	125mph (200km/h) – 4.6 V8 (1998 models)
	122mph (196km/h) – 4.6 V8 (1999 models)
0–60mph:	13.3sec – diesel manual
	14.7sec – diesel automatic
	9.9sec – 4.0 V8 manual
	10.4sec – 4.0 V8 automatic (1998 models)
	11.4sec – 4.0 V8 automatic (1999 models)
	9.3sec – 4.6 V8 (1998 models)
	9.6sec – 4.6 V8 (1999 models)

PAINT AND TRIM COMBINATIONS, 1998–1999 MODELS

Three types of paint were used on Range Rovers in this period: 'solid' paints (traditional standard types), 'metallic' paints (which incorporated tiny metal flakes to reflect light and give a higher sheen) and 'micatallic' paints (which incorporated tiny particles of mica to achieve a high sheen). All the metallic and micatallic paints used on Range Rovers had a clear protective coat applied over the colour coats, and these paints were known as 'clear-over-base' types.

Cloth upholstery was used for base models while leather was found on the more expensive variants.

1998 Model-Year (October 1997 to October 1998)

There were fourteen standard exterior colours for 1998, plus one special colour (Atlantis Blue) that was used only on the Vogue 50 limited edition in June 1998. Of the fourteen standard colours, six were new: Caledonian Blue, Chawton White, Cobar Blue, Rutland Red, White Gold and Woodcote Green. These replaced Arles Blue, Alpine White, Riviera Blue, Portofino Red, Avalon Blue and Willow Green respectively.

The four upholstery colours remained unchanged; Ash Grey, Granite Grey and Saddle Brown were available in both cloth and leather, but Lightstone Beige came only in leather. All types and colours were available with all standard exterior colours. Atlantis Blue paint came with special Parchment leather.

The Paint Colours

Altai Silver	Chawton White	Oxford Blue
Atlantis Blue	Cobar Blue	Rioja Red
Beluga Black	Coniston Green	Rutland Red
Caledonian Blue	Epsom Green	White Gold
Charleston Green	Niagara Grey	Woodcote Green

1999 Model-Year (October 1998 to September 1999)

There were fourteen exterior colours for the 1999 model-year, of which twelve were carried over from 1998. Two were direct replacements for 1998 season colours: Blenheim Silver, which replaced Altai Silver, and Java Black, which replaced Beluga Black.

There were three cloth colour options and four leather colour options. Cloth upholstery came in Ash Grey, Dark Granite or Walnut (which replaced Saddle). Leather upholstery came in Ash Grey, Dark Granite, Lightstone and Walnut. All types and colours were available with all exterior colours.

The Paint Colours

Blenheim Silver	Coniston Green	Rioja Red
Caledonian Blue	Epsom Green	Rutland Red
Charleston Green	Java Black	White Gold
Chawton White	Niagara Grey	Woodcote Green
Cobar Blue	Oxford Blue	

CHAPTER FOUR

REACHING FOR THE SKY

As the 2000 model-year opened in autumn 1999, Land Rover's marketing team was still driving the Range Rover relentlessly up-market to prepare the way for its replacement in 2001. So although there were visual changes to set the 2000 models apart from earlier models, the real focus was on increases in the luxury content.

Between its launch in autumn 1994 and the autumn of 1999, the Range Rover had been available with three levels of trim and equipment. Now a fourth and higher level was added (known internally as TL4). Special editions over the last couple of years had paved the way for this more expensive line-produced top model, to which a pair of even more expensive special editions drew attention as the new model-year opened.

In the UK, this new model was called the Range Rover Vogue, and it brought about a realignment of the range. While the entry-level 2.5 DT and 4.0 remained available,

both now renamed as County models, along with the SE and DSE, everything above that changed. So alongside the DHSE now came a 4.0 HSE, while the 4.6-litre engine was now offered only with the Vogue trim level as the flagship model.

The most obvious recognition features of the 2000 models were changes to the lights. The headlights now had 'masks', which gave the impression of two round lamps within the rectangular unit. (LRNA's President Charlie Hughes had suggested this even before 38A production had started, but he had been over-ruled on the grounds of cost!) Then the front indicators gained clear glass lenses with amber bulbs, and there were new clear glass side repeaters. There was smoked glass for the tail-lights as well, where the turn indicator and reversing light segments were blended into a single strip, giving a cleaner overall appearance. On models with front foglamps, the lenses of those lamps took on an elliptical graphic.

This 2000-model Range Rover displays the new front end with 'masked' headlamps and clear lenses for the indicators and wing-mounted repeaters. There is darkened 'privacy' glass behind the B-pillar, and the seats have the latest ruched leather. These are Hurricane alloy wheels.

A 2001 model, this time without the 'privacy' glass, and with the standard six-pleat style of upholstery.

NICK DIMBLEBY

The 'masked' headlamps used on the 2000 and later models. There are amber bulbs behind the clear turn indicator lenses.

A high-specification diesel model was now part of the regular showroom line-up.

Some cosmetic changes came across from the Autobiography range, too, so all front spoilers and mirror heads were now painted to match the body, and the tailgate release button was chromed. Mud-flaps became a standard fit right across the range, as did blue-tinted electro-chromic glass for the door mirrors: made by Schott, it dimmed automatically to prevent dazzle from lights behind the vehicle. Despite all these changes, there was actually not a lot to distinguish the top-model Vogue visually from other Range Rovers, although it did have its own plate badge on the tailgate, body-colour door handles, and bright inserts for the side rubbing strips. It also had a special bright finish for its Hurricane 18in wheels.

THE 2000 MODEL-YEAR

For the 2000 model-year, the UK market went its own way with wheel options. There were 16in Typhoons on the entry-level models, 16in Lightnings on the SE and DSE, and 18in Hurricanes with a standard finish on the HSE and DHSE. Although 18in wheels had been available as options for some years (and the Mondial and Triple Sport types still were), the 2000 model-year was the first time that any 18in wheel had become standard on a UK-market Range Rover. In other countries, the wheel selections differed. The USA made its own choices (see Chapter 5), but standard elsewhere were Futura wheels on entry-level models, Spyder wheels on SE and DSE, and Lightning wheels on the HSE derivatives.

Following on from the 1999 model-year changes, the aim of changes inside the passenger cabin had been to improve the feel and look to give a more luxurious ambiance. So a part-wood steering wheel became optional for all except the entry-level models, and the chrome package was imported from the Autobiography scheme, bringing chrome for the H-gate surround, the handbrake button and the auto-shift release button. Keeping up with the current Discovery, an additional power socket was also added in the rear loadspace, and an auto-dimming rear-view mirror was standardized.

Even the instruments and the clock changed for 2000, having green faces in place of the earlier white, and a useful graphic to remind the driver which side of the vehicle the fuel filler was on! Then the underside of the cubby box lid had cupholders on all models – two standard-size holders and two larger ones, mainly to suit North American buyers. Shortly after the start of the 2000 model-year, twin pop-out cupholders were added to the rear centre armrest on all except the entry-level models.

However, the major passenger cabin changes were reserved for the Vogue models. There were now seven colour choices of RV95 luxury-grade carpet, Classic Green, Prussian Blue and Rowan Berry Red being added to the four standard colours. Seat piping was chosen to match the carpet if Lightstone leather was specified, and the options were Classic Green, Prussian Blue and Old Red. The cubby box lid and the sides of the centre console were coordinated with the main interior colour, and there was extra wood trim. However, the wood was not all solid wood: it was actually wood foil with a burr walnut effect on the centre console, the window switch plate and the rear ashtray lid, chosen because it gave a more uniform colour match. Final touches were pre-wiring to accept a mobile telephone, an enhanced harmon/kardon ICE system with digital sound processing, and improved speakers. The result was a sound quality that Land Rover believed was equal to the best available in the luxury sector.

The 2000 model-year also brought a new choice of luxury options. A new fashion was for darkened 'privacy' glass behind the B-pillars, and so a 3mm glass with a 44 per cent tint became available for the Range Rover. There was also a new 'Oxford' ruched leather trim option, available on all except the entry-level models in the standard four colours. This was actually much more than its name suggested, in fact being a complete interior package, which included redesigned seats. These had a polywool interlay and a thicker,

The part-wood steering-wheel rim seen on this 2001 model was an option that came over from the Autobiography programme. The light-coloured leather upholstery has contrasting dark piping. NICK DIMBLEBY

softer foam that enhanced the softer leather. The leather itself was of a higher quality than the standard Range Rover type, and was used on the seat facings, door armrests, door-casing inserts, cubby box lid and handbrake gaiter. The rear seats of the 'Oxford' option had been reshaped to emphasize the four-seat configuration, and there was no contrasting piping.

It was now possible to order a satellite navigation system (at extra cost) outside the Autobiography programme, too. In fact, the latest Philips CARiN II+ was an improvement over the last version available through the Autobiography programme. It was integrated with the top-level ICE system, so that the two could not be bought separately. The system's controls and a full colour LCD display were integrated into a single dashboard unit, and CARiN II+ could also be used off-road, which was a first in the motor industry. The whole system came with a part-wood steering wheel that incorporated fingertip remote controls, and all the hardware was packed into the right-hand side of the loadspace. It consisted of the GPS receiver, a CD drive, and an associated computer. An updated CD-ROM was supplied free after six months, but further updates came at extra cost.

Although the 2000 model-year was punctuated by its fair share of special editions (see below) there were no running changes of significance to the specifications announced in October 1999. There was a minor enhancement, though: from March 2000, another 18in wheel style with 8in rim became available alongside the Mondial as a line-fit option and the Triple Sport as an accessory fit. This one featured polished flat spokes and was known as the Comet type.

Then, as the summer approached, a European Commission report on car pricing flagged up a major discrepancy between prices in the UK and prices in countries sharing the Euro currency. The report claimed that pre-tax prices were 34 per cent higher in the UK, and this news swiftly led to demands for price harmonization. Land Rover quickly complied, and on 25 July 2000, Land Rover prices were reduced across the board: Range Rover County prices were slashed by £1,375, and Vogue prices by £995. Land Rover UK's Managing Director, Mike Wright, explained his company's stance in these words:

> There has been a great deal of uncertainty in the UK market. We want to offer something genuine and permanent to our customers, and a straight no-nonsense price cut, allied to higher specification levels, is the best way to do it.

This was not the only price adjustment that would follow this report, either: there would be further reductions later.

The 2000 Special Editions

A new policy was in place by the time the 2000 model-year's special editions were rolled out. The manufacturing system had been streamlined to a degree, so that special editions were designed to have an appeal in multiple markets rather than in just one. This meant that LRSV could, in principle, build larger quantities of vehicles to a common specification,

which reduced cost and complication on the manufacturing side.

While the new line-production Vogue model planted the Range Rover firmly at a higher price point, a very special limited edition was announced at the start of the model-year with a £100,000 price tag – more than twice as much as any other model except the Vogue. The purpose of the Linley edition was really to see what the market might accept in terms of exclusivity and cost, but it also had the 'halo' effect of drawing attention to the Range Rover's move into a higher price bracket. Few were sold – though that was not really the point, and in any case Land Rover had always promised not to make more than ten examples in order to preserve their exclusivity.

Also announced in October 1999 was the Holland & Holland special edition, which was priced well above the top-model Vogue but, of course, lower than the Linley. In practice, the Holland & Holland did not become available until March 2000, when it gave a fillip to top-end sales partway through the season. And after an announcement in March, a third special edition became available in June, this one celebrating thirty years of the Range Rover brand and called the 30th Anniversary edition. Its pricing was pitched mid-way between the Vogue and the Holland & Holland – although with the addition of extras it came close to the more expensive of those two models.

The 2000 Global Limited Editions

Linley (October 1999)

The idea of the Linley edition came from Mike Gould, who had recently left LRSV as the marketing manager in charge of the Autobiography scheme. It gained headlines when it was announced at the London Motor Show on 20 October 1999 because of its £100,000 price tag, which was certainly partly justified by the amount of extra work that went into it, but was primarily a marketing ploy. That price was later dropped to £96,995 when prices were reduced on other Range Rovers in February 2001.

In theory, the Linley remained available to special order until the very end of second-generation Range Rover production in December 2001, always based on a top-model Vogue. Land Rover guaranteed its exclusivity by promising to build no more than around ten vehicles for world-wide markets, though in practice there were only ever six. Five had right-hand drive, and the sixth was a left-hand-drive

The all-black Linley edition was created in conjunction with Viscount Linley, who was pictured with it at the model's launch. NICK DIMBLEBY

The Linley had a special tailgate badge, of course.

The interior of the Linley was also all in black. Note the distinctive star-shaped inlay in the wood of the cubby box lid, and the Linley name on the dashboard rail. NICK DIMBLEBY

model built for the USA; four were sold in Britain, including the prototype, which was promptly stolen and has never been seen since.

This limited edition took its name from David Linley, a leading furniture designer who is also the Queen's nephew. Asked to come up with ideas for a very exclusive Range Rover and to put his name to it, he proposed an all-black model that would reflect the themes of his 'Metropolitan' range of furniture.

Each Range Rover Linley underwent 100 hours of hand finishing at Land Rover Special Vehicles. The vehicles were hand sprayed in solid black paint by XK Engineering in Coventry (a regular LRSV sub-contractor), and equipped with 'shadowchrome' finish 18in Hurricane alloy wheels finished with black highlights. The tailgate carried a 'Linley' plate badge.

The whole interior was finished in black, with leather used not only in the usual places, but also on the headlining and parcel shelf. The wood veneer trim was also in piano black, with stainless-steel etching in a 'starburst' graphic. This unique wood treatment was also used for the rear picnic tables, centre console surround, and the navigation and TV-video system with its twin monitor screens mounted in the back of the front seat headrests.

Holland & Holland (March 2000)

Like the earlier Holland & Holland Range Rovers for France and Belgium, this special edition was created in tandem with the sporting gunmaker. However, this one was built by Land Rover Special Vehicles at Solihull, and incorporated many additional features that reflected the gunmaker's products.

There were 100 Holland & Holland models for the UK, plus a further 300 for the USA. The edition was announced on 26 October 1999, but sales did not begin until March 2000. Each example was based on a 4.6 Vogue, which then underwent thirty hours of special finishing by Land Rover Special Vehicles. All exterior panels, including the body kit and radiator grille, were sprayed in unique Tintern Green, and the spokes of the bright-finish 18in Hurricane alloy wheels were given Tintern Green accents.

The interior was given a very distinctive 'country sports' feel through the use of Autobiography-style, Cheshire-grade, dark brown Bridle leather with Bridle accent piping on the seats. The dashboard, centre console, door cappings and rear picnic tables had a complete Autobiography wood kit in French-American walnut veneer with a gunstock grain,

The Holland & Holland was launched at the gunmaker's own sports ground near London, with singing star Ronan Keating in attendance.

The deep Tintern Green paint of the Holland & Holland edition was matched by accents on the wheels.

The interior matched matt 'gunstock' wood with dark brown leather to striking effect. NICK DIMBLEBY

The wood rail on the dashboard carried a discreet reminder that this was a special edition. This is a left-hand-drive example. NICK DIMBLEBY

Interior door handles were added to replicate the ornate metalwork of a Holland & Holland sporting gun, an example of which can be seen here. NICK DIMBLEBY

The kick plates on the sills were unique to the Holland & Holland edition...

developed especially for the Holland & Holland. There were also specially crafted interior door handles with character-istic Holland & Holland engraving, and a special picnic table was stowed in the load space.

The Holland & Holland edition was priced at £63,495, and twenty of the UK examples were built with twin rear TV screens and a video player, which cost £5,000 extra.

... as, of course, was the badge on the tailgate. NICK DIMBLEBY

30th Anniversary (June 2000)

The prototype 30th Anniversary Range Rover was shown at the Geneva Motor Show in March 2000, as this special edition was to be sold in several countries. Sales then began in June, exactly thirty years after the launch of the original Range Rover. So although the prototype was based on a 2000-model 4.6 Vogue, the production examples were based on 2001-model 4.6 Vogue Range Rovers. The new limited edition was shown to UK buyers for the first time at the NEC Motor Show in October, and UK sales started that month. There were examples for the USA and for Japan, too, although quantities are not known.

Just 100 were made for the UK, the first fifty priced at £57,500, while the second batch of fifty cost an additional £6,000 to cover extra equipment. This extra equipment consisted of twin TV screens fitted in the rear of the front seat headrests, a DVD player, privacy glass to the rear of the B posts, and additional Burr Maple veneer for the instrumentation and rear seat picnic tables. The showroom price of the 30th Anniversary models was lowered in February 2001, when Range Rover prices were lowered across the board in the UK. However, by that stage relatively few examples remained unsold.

All 30th Anniversary Range Rovers had distinctive Wimbledon Green paintwork – a colour taken from the Autobiography colour palette – and their bumpers, aprons, sills and door mirror heads were painted to match. The tailgate carried a special '30th Anniversary' plate badge, and the wheels were 18in bright-finish Hurricane alloys.

The seats were finished in Classic Green leather (again taken from the Autobiography options list) with Lightstone piping, and Lightstone was also found on the door trims and other interior hardware. The handbrake grip, gearshift and door-pull handles were trimmed in Classic Green leather, and the steering wheel was trimmed in duotone Classic Green and Lightstone. The door-lock escutcheons were chromed, and the wood trim was in Burr Maple with an amber stain.

As an aside, it appears that an early intention was to make the 30th Anniversary edition available in two colours: Highland Green and Carmen Pearl. Carmen Pearl had been reserved for special edition use, and was used for the Discovery MM or Millennium edition in January 2000. However, when a further batch of the MM was called for in May, supplies of Carmen Pearl paint had run out, and the additional models were finished in Alveston Red instead. So the

The 30th Anniversary edition was painted in Wimbledon Green and featured dark green upholstery with contrasting piping.

The tailgate carried a reminder that the 30th Anniversary Range Rover was something special... NICK DIMBLEBY

... and in case passengers needed reminding, the details were repeated on special sill panels.

likelihood is that Carmen Pearl disappeared from the 30th Anniversary edition specification for the same reason. Why Highland Green gave way to Wimbledon Green is not clear.

The 2000 Swiss Limited Edition

Unable to secure an allocation of the 30th Anniversary edition that was built for the UK and USA, Land Rover's Swiss National Sales Company created its own.

The Swiss 30th Anniversary edition came in two col-ours: Epsom Green or Wimbledon Green. It was otherwise broadly similar to the UK 30th Anniversary model, with body-colour mirrors and bumpers, 18in bright-finish Hurricane wheels, and a special logo on the tailgate. The interior combined Lightstone trim with Classic Green seat surfaces and piping in the same way, with amber-tinted walnut wood trim, a duotone leather-trimmed steering wheel, chromed interior door handles, and Classic Green carpets. The base model was a 4.6-litre Vogue, and a CARiN II GPS system was included in the price of 111,400CHF. It is not clear how many were made.

LAND ROVER SOLD TO FORD

The Land Rover marque had been owned by the German BMW car company since January 1994, but the relationship between the two companies had sometimes been an uneasy one. BMW had also been unable to turn the loss-making Rover Cars business unit into a revenue earner, and in 2000 the patience of the German company's Board finally wore thin.

After a boardroom coup, the decision was taken to sell Rover Cars and Land Rover as separate entities. Rover went to a business consortium in Britain, while Land Rover was snapped up by Ford and formally became part of that American empire on 1 July 2000. In due course, Land Rover would become part of Ford's Premier Automotive Group.

The change of ownership had no discernible effect on the 38A Range Rover, as the plans for its final two seasons of production (the 2001 and 2002 model-years) were already set in stone. As part of the deal with Ford, BMW undertook to complete outstanding work on the third-generation Range Rover and to supply components for the forthcoming new model as originally planned. There was, though, one interesting change: the project code was changed from L30 to L322, which harmonized better with the Ford system.

THE TREK RANGE ROVER

The TReK competition started in the USA as a means of encouraging team spirit within Land Rover dealerships (for more about it, *see* Chapter 5). For 2001 it became a global event, and dealer teams from the UK were also entered. However, the whole event attracted very little publicity in the UK.

The 2001 event was held in South Africa. The dealer teams used specially prepared Series II Discoverys, but LRSV also prepared a single right-hand-drive Range Rover for the event management team. This was a 2000-model 4.0 SE, painted in the event's characteristic orange and black colours and equipped with a number of off-road accessories. There is a story that two other similar vehicles, both with left-hand-drive, were prepared for overseas publicity purposes, but their existence has never been confirmed.

Just one RHD Range Rover was built for TReK 2001, painted in the Molten Orange and Black colours associated with the event. It still survives, in the hands of an enthusiast. JÉRÔME ANDRÉ

The black wheels suit the colour scheme well. Note the special roofrack and access ladder here. JÉRÔME ANDRÉ

THE 2001 MODEL-YEAR

With the launch of the third-generation Range Rover just eighteen months away, it is no surprise that the changes made for the 2000 model-year were the last major ones to the 38A model. The paint and interior trim choices remained unchanged for 2001, and the only change of any real note was that the Vogue models now took on satellite navigation as a standard feature.

Behind the scenes, though, some interesting plans for the 38A's future were under discussion at Solihull. These centred on whether to keep the model in production for a limited period to cover the transition to the new third-generation L322. The anticipated new Range Rover was going to represent a step-change much like the one that 38A itself had represented in 1994, and at that time the old model had

been kept in production as the Range Rover Classic to ease the transition.

Critical in these discussions was the pricing strategy for the forthcoming new model, which was to be introduced with an attractively low entry-level price. If the 38A was to remain available alongside the new model, it would have to be cheaper – and the only realistic way of making it cheaper while keeping it profitable was to delete some of its more expensive equipment.

So a team at Land Rover began to look at ways of delivering a stripped-out 38A that was still luxurious enough to be called a Range Rover and was still well enough specified to justify its pricing above the top-level Discoverys. It was a tall order, but one of the options that gained serious consideration was to fit it with conventional steel coil springs in place of the air springs it had had since the beginning. It might have worked – but there was little enthusiasm from the dealer network for a stripped-out 38A, which would, of course, have hit second-hand prices quite badly. So the idea was dropped, and this time there would be a clean break with the outgoing model when the new one was introduced.

Other issues at the time also had an effect on this thinking. The problem of cheaper European imports that Land Rover had tried to address with price reductions in the summer of 2000 did not go away, and on 20 February 2001 the company announced that it would be slashing the prices of every Range Rover model by £3,000. (It was in fact £3,005 on petrol models and £3,010 on diesels, the difference being accounted for by an extra £5 Vehicle Excise Duty on diesels under the latest graduated scheme.) This brought the entry-level price of Range Rover ownership down to £36,995, while the HSE now cost £42,995 and the top-model Vogue was £49,995. These reduced prices, which also affected the

limited editions then on sale, certainly reduced Land Rover's room for manoeuvre with a stripped-out 38A.

Supplier problems now began to affect Range Rover specifications. If the model had been destined for a longer time in production, no doubt the company would have sought alternative suppliers to fill the gaps, but as it was they did not. So from 23 January 2001, the electro-chromic door mirrors were deleted from the HSE, DHSE and Vogue models, and were no longer available even as an option. At the same time, the rear courtesy spot and puddle lamps on the rear doors were deleted from the HSE and DHSE. Not long afterwards, on 1 March, Ash Grey cloth seats became unavailable, the result of what Land Rover described as 'supplier constraints'.

Despite this apparent retrenchment, sales were still holding up. First-quarter sales of Range Rovers in the UK were reported to be 4 per cent up over the same period in 2000. On 18 May, Land Rover announced that UK Range

Body-coloured accents on the wheels were used again to good effect on the Bordeaux edition.

Rover sales for the year to date were up by a massive 41 per cent as compared to the previous year, and that the most expensive Vogue model was proving the best-seller. In July, the company announced that UK sales of 2,134 Range Rovers in the first six months of the year represented an increase of 10 per cent over the comparable period in 2000. Although it is hard to reconcile these claims and figures, they do make clear that the 38A Range Rover was still a strong sales proposition as it approached its last months in production.

Over the summer period, sales were further supported by a pair of limited-edition models in the UK, plus one locally prepared special edition in France. Both of the UK editions, the Bordeaux and the Westminster, were deliberately targeted at strong-selling competitor vehicles.

The 2001 UK Limited Editions
Bordeaux (June 2001)

The 200-strong Bordeaux limited edition was introduced on 28 June 2001 to give Land Rover a product in the under £40,000 sector, and a competitor for the new Mercedes-Benz ML430. Based on the entry-level County model, its on-the-road price was £38,995. There were 100 4.0-litre petrol and 100 2.5-litre turbodiesel models, all with automatic transmission and an electric sunroof.

All the Bordeaux models were finished in wine-coloured Alveston Red, with the bumpers, sills and door mirror heads painted to match. There were also Alveston Red highlights on the spokes of the 18in Proline alloy wheels. The interior was upholstered in Lightstone leather, with Rowan Berry

The Westminster edition promoted the new Bonatti Grey colour for the 2002 season. JOHN CARTER

Red piping on the edges of the seats and matching carpets. The steering wheel, door trims, handbrake gaiter and gear-shift knob were all in Lightstone leather.

Westminster (August 2001)

Although the Westminster limited edition was announced on 26 February 2001 at the Geneva Motor Show, deliveries to customers did not begin until August 2001. There were 200 examples in all, 150 based on the 4.0 SE and the other fifty on the 2.5 DSE. In each case, the showroom price was £46,495 – a figure set deliberately to target potential buyers of the BMW X5.

The Westminster was designed to be restrained and practical. Its name suggested the high public profile associated with the heart of British politics, while its colour schemes reflected the sobriety of a traditional business suit. There were just three paint options – Blenheim Silver, Bonatti Grey and Java Black – and the bumpers and sills were painted to match the body. The wheels were 18in Hurricane alloys with a gunmetal finish and 255/55R18 tyres, and the tailgate carried a 'Westminster' plate badge.

The interior colours were sober and restrained, too: every Westminster had Ash Grey leather upholstery with Charcoal piping and unique grey Poplar Anthracite wood trim, while the carpets in the cabin, in the boot and on the tailgate were all in Ash Grey. Front door sill plates bearing the Westminster name were an attractive touch.

Other standard features included an electric sunroof and front seats with electric height adjustment. Westminsters had satellite navigation with a TrafficMaster monitor system, and an enhanced in-car entertainment system with seventeen speakers. These were the twelve of the Vogue's system, plus an extra five: two tweeters in the rear doors, two surround speakers in the rear quarter-panels, and a 'centre-fill' speaker mounted in the middle of the dashboard, where it replaced the standard oddments tray.

The 2001 French Limited Edition

Known as the Aspen, this French limited edition became available in June 2001 with two levels of trim; the plain Aspen was matched by an Aspen Pack version. Both came in Blenheim Silver, Bonatti Grey, Java Black or Oslo Blue, with Aspen side decals. Upholstery was in Ash Grey or Lightstone, and there was a K7 radio with a CD changer in

The Westminster had a number of special features. The tailgate badge was one of them...

... the 'centre-fill' speaker on the dashboard was another....

... and then, of course, there was the special wood trim as well.

the boot, and steering-wheel controls. The Aspen had 16in Lightning wheels and cost 319,500FF with either the 4.0-litre V8 or the 2.5-litre diesel engine.

The Aspen Pack added 18in Proline wheels, body-colour spoiler and mirror heads, rear privacy glass, headlamp washers, chromed inserts in the side bump strips, and front fog lights (on V8s only). It came with a heated windscreen and electrically adjustable heated front seats. With these extras,

it cost 359,500FF with either engine. For comparison, a 4.0 SE or a 2.5 DSE then cost 358,500FF.

THE FINAL MODELS: THE 2002 MODEL-YEAR

The 2001 model-year was the last one that the 38A Range

WHAT THE PRESS THOUGHT

[The Range Rover] looks considerably better with the recently introduced smoked indicators and tail-lights, and better still when finished in a nice sombre metallic... [but] the build quality is variable and shutlines are big, most noticeably the black void between bumper and tailgate. And the nearside door mirror glass fell out on our test car, and then neatly popped back in.
(*Car*, March 2001)

Over the years, minor tweaks such as colour-coding the bumpers and fitting much more stylish alloy wheels have improved the Range Rover's appearance. Early ones look very ordinary compared to the latest models. But I still don't think the styling has anything like the individuality and distinction of the original Range Rover.

The 4.6-litre engine has come on a long way since the first production examples in 1994. All the early ones I tried were more urgent-sounding – even a little raucous – and I was never particularly impressed with the acceleration they delivered. The latest version seems to give much better motorway flexibility from its re-shaped torque curve.... Even fuel economy has improved.

The whole vehicle feels like a great big wobbly jelly at times (try one at speed over a succession of potholes and you'll see what I mean), and the steering feels woolly.

Acceleration [from the diesel engine] for overtaking is a long time in coming, and there were many occasions during my time with the DHSE when I found the thing embarrassingly slow.... As for fuel economy, the best I could manage was 22mpg on a long run.
(*Land Rover Enthusiast*, August 2001)

The [4.6-litre] engine sometimes sounds just a little strained under hard acceleration... but it doesn't feel as if it's being overworked, since the big car simply leaps forward when the accelerator is floored.

Many [buyers] are quite prepared to overlook the expense of purchasing and owning a Range Rover simply because it's still the car for seriously rich people to be seen in.
(*4×4*, August 2001)

It's hard to believe that you're driving such a big car, the accelerative response is so eager, the steering so lively.

What really makes the Range Rover Vogue is the traditional wood and leather trim.
(*Land Rover World*, October 2001)

The 30th Anniversary model's combination of Classic Green leather with Lightstone piping and amber Burr Maple wood trim works very well. It makes the driver and passengers feel as if they really are being treated like lords. Special kick-plates reading '30th Anniversary' provide a unique welcoming touch, too, while chromed interior handles and sill button surrounds are subtleties which make more of a difference than you might expect. You're left in no doubt that this is a luxury car as the 4.6-litre V8 wafts you along with a commendable absence of intrusive noise.
(*Land Rover Enthusiast*, May 2003)

The flat-spoke Comet alloy wheels on a very late 2002 model. NICK DIMBLEBY

Rover had to itself. Even though a 2002 model-year of sorts was announced at the Frankfurt Motor Show that opened on 11 September 2001, the first pictures of the new L322 model were sent to the media together with outline information in November. The new Range Rover was introduced at a special event held in the Design Museum in London that month before an invited audience, and actual sales were announced as starting on 15 February. Further details were issued to the media in December, and a ride-and-drive event followed at Skibo Castle in Scotland early in the New Year. Meanwhile, Land Rover dealers and company personnel were introduced to the new model at a special event based at Lake Garda in Italy, and in January the model made its public debut at the Detroit International Motor Show.

So against that background of mounting expectation, the 38A held the fort with some final special editions, but with minimal changes to the mainstream models. There were two changes in the colour palette, and the HSE and DHSE models lost their wood-and-leather steering wheel option, which was now only available as part of the standard Vogue specification. The Vogue also exchanged its earlier Hurricane alloy wheels for Comet six-spoke alloys with a chrome effect, still running on the same 255/55R18 tyres. Meanwhile the range was trimmed, as the manual gearbox option was dropped from the diesel County (although it could be had to special order).

In the UK, all the interest was really centred on the limited-edition Vogue SE that was introduced at Motor Show time, and acted as a high-specification run-out edition. Some examples of the Bordeaux and the Westminster no doubt still lingered in the showrooms, but probably not for long. Then there was a final special edition for Scotland only, called the Braemar and released in November 2001. This was part of a regional strategy rather than an integral part

The final 38A model leaves the assembly line in December 2001, with the original programme
director John Hall driving, and Spen King (who had designed the first Range Rover) beside him.

of Land Rover's global run-out strategy for the 38A Range
Rover.

The end came at 3pm on 13 December 2001, when the last
second-generation Range Rover was driven off the assembly
lines in Solihull's North Block during a special ceremony. In
the driving seat was John Hall, the man who had directed the
project to develop it, and alongside him in the passenger seat
was Spen King, father of the original or classic Range Rover.

Reflecting the importance to the 38A Range Rover of the
North American market, that last-of-line model was a North
American specification 4.6 HSE (see Chapter 5). It was on
chassis number SALPM16412A-467128, and was finished in
Alveston Red with Lightstone leather interior. According to
Land Rover's own calculations, it was the 167,401st example
of the 38A to be built.

At a special ceremony in February 2002, the last 38A

was handed over into the keeping of the Heritage Motor
Museum, along with the first production example of the
third-generation Range Rover. However, just over a year
later, in June 2003, it was auctioned off to the highest
bidder when the Heritage Motor Museum needed to weed
its collection to make space for a broader selection of
vehicles. Its new owner paid £33,925 for it. Since then,
it has found its way to the famous Dunsfold Collection in
Surrey.

The 2002 UK Limited Editions

Vogue SE (September 2001)

This fourth and last Vogue SE edition was based on the 4.6-
litre Vogue. It was priced to combat the 4.4-litre version of

The last-of-line model was built to NAS specification, but remained in the UK and was given a 2002 registration number. It now belongs to the Dunsfold Collection.

the BMW X5, and to pre-empt the forthcoming Mercedes-Benz ML500. Production began in September 2001.

There were 300 examples, which came in four colours, as shown in the table below. Bumpers and sills were painted to match the body, and all examples came with fog lamps. The wheels were 18in Comet alloys, and there was a Vogue SE tailgate badge.

Lightstone leather upholstery was standard, with piping to match the exterior paint. Carpets were also chosen to complement the paint, being Red with Alveston Red, Green with Epsom Green, Lightstone with Java Black, and Blue with Oslo Blue. Door grabs, handbrake gaiter and gearshift knob were all in Lightstone, while the steering wheel was in plain Ash Grey with all interior colours. (The original plan had

been to have a duotone wheel, colour coded to match the seat piping, but this was abandoned at the last minute.)

The wood trim was unique to this final Vogue SE, being in burr walnut with highlights in Classic Green, Grand Black, Prussian Blue or Rowan Berry Red to match the exterior colour.

Additional equipment as compared to the Vogue models were the TrafficMaster monitor system and seventeen-speaker ICE, both as seen in the Westminster limited edition. Of the 300 Vogue SEs built, fifty were equipped with an 'option pack' of twin wide-screen TVs and a DVD system for the rear seat passengers, plus privacy glass to the rear of the B-posts. The 'ordinary' Vogue SE cost £53,995, and models with the TV-DVD system and privacy glass cost £57,995.

The Braemar edition was sold only in Scotland, at the start of the 2002 season.

Breakdown of the Build of this Final Limited Edition

	SE	SE with DVD	Total
Alveston Red	35	7	42
Epsom Green	63	13	76
Java Black	60	12	72
Oslo Blue	92	18	110
Total	250	50	300

Braemar (November 2001)

The Range Rover Braemar was launched at the Scottish Motor Show on 9 November 2001, in tandem with Braemar editions of the Discovery, Defender and Freelander.

Available only through Land Rover dealers in Scotland and created specifically for them, the twenty-five Braemar models consisted of fifteen examples based on the DHSE and ten based on the HSE. Both versions had an on-the-road price of £42,995. The Braemar was painted in Blenheim Silver and had Ash Grey leather upholstery with picnic tables, privacy glass and play stations for the rear-seat passengers.

There were identifying badges on the wings as well as the tailgate of the Braemar.

The 2002 Japanese Limited Edition

To mark the end of 38A production, the Japanese National Sales Company offered a special edition called the Range Rover Royal Edition. This was based on a 4.6-litre HSE (still the top specification in Japan) and had Epsom Green paint. The name supposedly came from the fact that Range Rovers supplied to the British royal family were also usually in dark green. The build total for this edition is not known.

The interior was in Lightstone, with additional wood trim. Seats and the footwell mats were both piped in green. The latest DVD-based satellite navigation system was also standard, and the model came with Hurricane alloy wheels. Each Range Rover had a script decal reading 'Royal Edition' below its 4.6 HSE tailgate badge, and each one also came with a special green leather key fob with a plate reading 'Range Rover Royal Edition'.

EPILOGUE

That total of 167,401 second-generation Range Rovers seems remarkably small by modern motor industry standards, and helps to emphasize that in global terms this was a low-volume model. Some commentators might be prepared to argue that this low total contributes to its exclusivity.

The production total also demands comment from another perspective: 167,401 is barely more than half of the 317,615 that was the total Land Rover claimed for the first-generation Range Rover. But the overall totals tend to conceal the reality: the original Range Rover reached that total over a period of twenty-five and a half years, which gives an average annual production of 12,455 vehicles. The 38A was in production for just seven and a half years, which gives an average annual production of 22,320.

Quite clearly, Land Rover had got something right – and the new L322 would build on the solid foundations laid down by its two predecessors.

PAINT AND TRIM COMBINATIONS, 2000–2002 MODELS

2000 Model-Year (October 1999 to September 2000)

There were fourteen standard exterior colours, of which eleven were carried over from 1999. The three new ones were Alveston Red (which replaced Rioja Red), Icelandic Blue (instead of Charleston Green) and Kent Green (in place of Woodcote Green). One additional colour, Tintern Green, was used only on the Holland & Holland limited edition.

There were now four cloth upholstery colour options and four leather colour options. Cloth upholstery came in Ash Grey, Dark Granite, Darkstone Beige or Walnut. Leather upholstery came in Ash Grey, Dark Granite, Lightstone and Walnut. All types and colours were available with all exterior colours, but the piping on leather seats varied to suit the exterior colour.

The Paint Options

Alveston Red	Coniston Green	Niagara Grey
Blenheim Silver	Epsom Green	Oxford Blue
Caledonian Blue	Icelandic Blue	Rutland Red
Chawton White	Java Black	Tintern Green
Cobar Blue	Kent Green	White Gold

WHEEL STYLES, 2000–2002 MODELS

2000 Model-Year

The standard wheel styles were now the Mirage (entry-level), Lightning (SE) and Hurricane (HSE). The new Vogue model had a bright-finish version of the Hurricane wheel. The Mirage wheel was in fact the same as the earlier Stratos type, but with a new name. Mondial and Triple Sport styles remained available, the latter still as an accessory fit only. Comet wheels became an option from March 2000.

Mirage	Five-spoke	8×16
Comet	Six-spoke	8×18

2001 Model-Year

The standard wheels remained the same as for the 2000 model-year. Proline 18in wheels reappeared for special editions in summer 2001, after being withdrawn for Range Rover use while demand for them as a Discovery Series II option was met.

Proline	Five-spoke	8×18

2001 Model-Year (October 2000 to September 2001)

All fourteen standard exterior colours were carried over from the 2000 model-year. A fifteenth colour, Bonatti Grey, was available only on the Westminster special edition.

The interior options were also carried over from the 2000 model-year. However, Ash Grey cloth upholstery was delisted from 1 March 2001.

2002 Model-Year (September 2001 to February 2002)

The total number of exterior paint options dropped to thirteen as Cobar Blue was deleted, but two of these were new colours – Vienna Green and Zambezi Silver.

There were now three cloth upholstery colour options and four leather colour options. Cloth upholstery came in Ash Grey, Granite Grey, or Walnut. Leather upholstery came in Ash Grey, Dark Granite, Lightstone and Walnut. All types and colours could be had with all exterior colours, but as supplies ran down towards the end of production it is likely that some combinations became unavailable.

The Paint Options

Alveston Red	Icelandic Blue	Vienna Green
Caledonian Blue	Java Black	White Gold
Chawton White	Niagara Grey	Zambezi Silver
Coniston Green	Oxford Blue	
Epsom Green	Rutland Red	

2002 Model-Year

The only change for the short 2002 model-year was that the formerly optional Comet alloy wheels replaced the bright-finish Hurricane type as the standard fit for Vogue models.

Comet 18in wheel.

TECHNICAL SPECIFICATIONS, 2000–2002 MODELS

Engines:

2.5-litre diesel

BMW M51 6-cylinder diesel with cast-iron block and light-alloy head

2497cc (80 × 82.8mm)

Single overhead camshaft

Seven-bearing crankshaft

Indirect injection with turbocharger and intercooler

Compression ratio 22:1

136bhp at 4,400rpm

197lb/ft at 2,000rpm

4.0-litre V8

Land Rover V8-cylinder petrol with alloy block and cylinder heads

3947cc (93.98 × 71.1mm)

Single overhead camshaft

Five-bearing crankshaft

Bosch injection with Motronic 5.2.1 electronic engine-management system

Compression ratio 9.38:1

185bhp at 4,750rpm

250lb/ft at 2,600rpm

4.6-litre V8

Land Rover V8-cylinder petrol with alloy block and cylinder heads

4554cc (93.98 × 82mm)

Single overhead camshaft

Five-bearing crankshaft

Bosch injection with Motronic 5.2.1 electronic engine-management system

Compression ratio 9.38:1

218bhp at 4,750rpm

294lb/ft at 2,600rpm

Primary gearbox:

Manual (2.5 diesel)

Five-speed, type R380

Ratios 3.69:1, 2.13:1, 1.40:1, 1.00:1, 0.73:1, reverse 3.53:1

Automatic (2.5 diesel and 4.0 petrol)

Four-speed, ZF 4HP22

Ratios 2.48:1, 1.48:1, 1.00:1, 0.73:1, reverse 2.09:1

Automatic (4.6 petrol)

Four-speed, ZF 4HP24 automatic

Ratios 2.48:1, 1.48:1, 1.00:1, 0.73:1, reverse 2.09:1

Transfer gearbox:
Two-speed Borg Warner type 13-61
Ratios 1.22:1 (high) and 3.27:1 (low)

All transfer gearboxes with self-locking viscous-coupled centre differential

Axle ratio:
3.54:1

Suspension:
Front and rear live axles with electronically controlled air springs and telescopic dampers; front axle located by cranked radius arms and Panhard rod, with anti-roll bar; rear axle located by composite trailing links and Panhard rod

Steering:
Recirculating-ball system with power assistance as standard; 17.5:1 ratio

Brakes:
Four-wheel disc brakes with dual hydraulic line, vacuum servo assistance and four-channel ABS; reverse-ventilated front discs with 11.7in diameter and four-piston calipers; solid rear discs with 12in diameter and two-piston calipers; separate internal expanding drum-type parking brake, operating on transmission output shaft

Dimensions:

Overall length:	185.6in (4,713mm)
Overall width:	74.4in (1,889mm)
Overall height:	71.6in (1,817mm) at standard ride height
Wheelbase:	108.1in (2,745mm)
Track, front:	60.6in (1,540mm)
Track, rear:	60.2in (1,530mm)

Wheels and tyres:
Various styles of five-bolt alloy wheel with 16in diameter and 7in or 8in rim; or with 18in diameter and 8in rim. Tyres with 235 or 255 section

Kerb weight (for typical UK-market models):
4,662lb (2,115kg) – diesel manual
4,695lb (2,130kg) – diesel automatic
4,630lb (2,100kg) – 4.0 V8 automatic
4,894lb (2,220kg) – 4.6 V8

Performance:

Max. speed:	105mph (170km/h) – diesel manual
	101mph (162km/h) – diesel automatic
	116mph (187km/h) – 4.0 V8 automatic
	122mph (196km/h) – 4.6 V8
0–60mph:	13.3sec – diesel manual
	14.7sec – diesel automatic
	11.4sec – 4.0 V8 automatic
	9.6sec – 4.6 V8

CHAPTER FIVE

THE NORTH AMERICAN MODELS

From the start of work on Project Discovery in 1988, Land Rover had seen sales in the USA as a very important factor in its business strategy for the new Range Rover. At that stage, the original Range Rover had been on sale there for only a year, but the early signs were encouraging. By the end of the 1980s, Range Rover sales were averaging around 4,000 vehicles a year, and although there were later fluctuations, this was clearly a healthy total. It was also one on which Land Rover was determined to build with the new Range Rover.

Land Rover's success in the USA had been exemplary. A small team had built up Range Rover sales from zero at the start of 1987, and had been able to create an image of exclusivity for the vehicle. Despite the age of the design – it was already seventeen years old when introduced to the USA – and despite a ride and build quality that were out of step with current expectations, it had caught the imagination of US buyers. By 1990, the USA had become the biggest single market for Range Rovers anywhere in the world, taking around 30 per cent of annual production. And although the actual numbers sold were tiny in US terms, they were very valuable to a small company such as Land Rover.

That was why Land Rover involved key members of its North American team throughout the development period of the 38A Range Rover. Charlie Hughes, President of what was originally called Range Rover of North America but became Land Rover North America in 1992, made regular visits to the UK to make his input to the programme. He would often be accompanied by other key members of his management team, and their views were instrumental in the creation of a Range Rover that would continue to sell around 30 per cent of its annual production in the USA. But that 30 per cent was of a much larger annual production total than in the days of the old model. North American sales of the 38A Range Rover would eventually average around 7,000 units a year.

North American buyers had only ever been offered Range Rovers with a high luxury specification, and so the entry-level types were not sold there. Nor were manual gearbox models or those with diesel engines; manual gearboxes were not considered appropriate for a luxury vehicle, and in the USA (though less so in Canada) diesel fuel was still perceived as belonging to trucks and therefore as being totally inconsistent with the Land Rover marque's luxury image.

US emissions and crash safety regulations of course had their effect on the vehicles sold there, and although Land Rover always did its best to minimize manufacturing differences by creating a globally acceptable specification, US models often had special features not seen elsewhere. This is why they had their own designation within Land Rover, being known as NAS (North American Specification) types. Generally speaking, Range Rovers for Canada followed the US lead, although all of them had their own differences (see sidebar).

RANGE ROVERS FOR CANADA

Range Rovers for Canada had essentially the same specifications as those for North America, except where otherwise noted. However, the Canadian models all had three distinctive differences to meet local conditions.

The first of these was a speedometer marked in kilometres per hour rather than miles per hour, to suit Canadian preferences. The second was daytime running lights – side and tail-lights that switched on automatically when the engine was started – to meet Canadian regulations. The third was an engine-block heater, to suit the extreme cold in certain parts of Canada. This could be plugged directly into a household electric mains system, and would warm the engine coolant to give easier starting in very cold conditions.

In addition, LRNA had its own special and limited-edition models to suit local market conditions, and its Callaway special edition in 1999 was a completely individual creation that was not made available outside the USA.

THE 1995 MODELS

The second-generation Range Rover was formally introduced to North American customers at the Detroit Motor Show in January 1995, although many potential customers would have been aware that it had been available in Europe for some months. Those months had allowed Land Rover to increase production at a comfortable rate so that the assembly lines were ready for the additional demand from North America, and in theory, the new Range Rover was available in showrooms immediately.

The NAS model range for 1995 was very straightforward. There was just one version of the 38A available, badged as a 4.0 SE. LRNA generally avoided the complication of calling it a 'new' Range Rover, instead encouraging customers and the media to see the 4.0 SE as a replacement for the discontinued County LWB model (known as the Vogue LSE in the UK), the former flagship of the range. A showroom price slightly above that of the County LWB, and several thousand dollars above the last of the old Range Rovers, now known as County Classic types, helped to make the necessary distinction.

Simplification was certainly the name of the game. There were only eight paint colours available, as against the fourteen offered in other markets, and only one of them was an extra-cost option. All except one colour also had the same single choice of upholstery colour, which helped to create a clear identity for the new model, and had the side benefit of simplifying things on the production lines at Solihull.

The first NAS models were all 4.0 SE types. However, as this picture shows, they had the five-spoke alloy wheels associated with the 4.6 HSE in other markets.

Even so, the 1995 NAS 4.0 SE was very different from a UK-market 4.0 SE. For a start, it was only available with an automatic gearbox. It also came as standard with an electric tilt-and-slide glass sunroof, and 16in Stratos five-spoke alloy wheels with 255/65 Michelin tyres, both items associated with the 4.6 HSE in the UK. Leather upholstery with heated front seats, and a two-position memory for the driver's seat and door mirrors, were features chosen from among the more luxurious ones on the 38A menu.

There were some unique features, too. One was the standard-fit ICE system that consisted of a Clarion 120-watt head unit with full electronic logic. Its radio could receive AM, FM and Weather Band, it incorporated a stereo cassette player, and it also controlled a six-CD autochanger. An eleven-speaker system was installed, again as part of the standard specification. A third brake light was standard at the bottom of the upper tailgate, where other models had only a blank in the trim. In both the USA and Canada, all new Range Rovers came with a three-year warranty from the start, extending to 42,000 miles in the USA, or 70,000km in metricated Canada. This was a better warranty than was available in the UK, where a three-year warranty would not be introduced until April 1998.

The new model got off to a flying start, selling just under 3,000 examples in the USA in the first six months of 1995. That implied full-year figures approaching 6,000, which was far better than even the best years of first-generation Range Rover sales in the USA. Although few people at LRNA can have imagined matching that figure on a regular basis, it did indicate that the customers liked what had been presented to them in the showroom, and promised big things for the future.

THE 1996 MODELS

For the last few months of 1995, the 4.0 SE remained the only variant of the 38A Range Rover on sale in the USA, accompanied in the showrooms by small numbers of the final County Classic variants of the first-generation model. Internal marketing documents from Land Rover also refer to a Lion special edition with Sahara Gold paint – possibly a way of selling examples with an unpopular colour – but there is no firm evidence that this ever went on sale. However, the round of US motor shows at the start of the new year would see the introduction of a 4.6 HSE model as well.

The US model strategy was very different from that

The 4.6-litre engine became available for 1996, here under the bonnet of a **NAS Range Rover.**

adopted in other countries. The addition of the 4.6 HSE gave LRNA a two-model Range Rover line-up again – but it had been shifted subtly higher up the price scale. A 4.6 HSE now cost $62,000 against the $55,000 of a 4.0 SE. Just over a year earlier, the old-model Range Rover in standard wheelbase form had cost a mere $45,000.

There were no changes to the 4.0 SE until the start of 1996, when some new paint options were introduced. However, when the 4.6 HSE arrived, it was made distinctively different, with 18in Mondial alloy wheels as standard. A chromed exhaust tip and mudflaps as standard further distinguished the bigger-engined variant, and of course there was a '4.6 HSE' tailgate badge. LRNA's promotional emphasis was on its performance, although it did not neglect the exclusivity brought about by a restricted range of paint and interior options. For that reason, some promotional material referred to it as a 'limited edition'.

Initial LRNA press releases suggested that the 4.6 HSE would be available in only two colours, but by April 1996 (if not earlier) there were three. Rioja Red was exclusive to the larger-engined model, as was the Ash Black upholstery available only with Beluga Black paint. The third option was Alpine White. All 4.6 HSE models also came with a Homelink system as standard. This was essentially a transmitter in the vehicle, which sent messages to a receiver in the owner's home. Activating the Homelink system from the car would switch the house lights on remotely just before the driver reached home. North American customers liked this feature, which had the advantage of making an empty house feel more welcoming, as well as scaring off any burglars who

SUPPORTING THE BRAND

When Land Rover North America was established in 1992, the company pioneered a new retail concept of themed, standalone dealerships called 'Land Rover Centres' (spelled the English way in honour of the brand's origins). The décor in these showrooms was carefully crafted to reflect Land Rover's heritage of exploration and adventure, and the employees all wore Land Rover-branded clothing to symbolize their commitment to the brand and its ethos.

From October 1996, LRNA also introduced Land Rover Kit and Land Rover Gear. This was essentially a rebranding exercise, Land Rover Kit being optional accessories for the vehicles and Land Rover Gear being a range of branded clothing that ranged from baseball caps through shirts and boots to luggage. Gear items generally used muted, earthy colours that were designed to reflect the outdoor heritage of the brand.

All this helped to strengthen the identity of the Land Rover brand in the USA and Canada, and provided valuable support for sales by allowing customers to imagine that they had joined an exclusive club when they bought a new Range Rover.

LRNA's Land Rover Centres followed a readily recognizable corporate design. This one was in Massapequa, on Long Island, east of New York City.

Land Rover Centres were designed to reinforce the idea that buying and owning a Land Rover product opened the door to exciting adventure.

might have decided that the owner of a 4.6 HSE was probably wealthy enough to have something worth stealing!

For the 1996 season, sales more than doubled over the 1995 returns for both the USA and Canada. It was clear that Land Rover and its North American sales company had got the product right.

THE 1997 MODELS

LRNA announced the 1997 Range Rovers on 14 October 1996. There were still just two models, 4.0 SE and 4.6 HSE, but changes were minimal. In line with Range Rovers for the rest of the world, the NAS models took on jewelled centre caps in their wheels, but they did not yet have the twin-

There were no major changes for the 1997 model-year: this is a 4.0 SE.

Although this is the interior of a 1997-model 4.0 SE, it has the wood fillets on the doors associated with the 4.6 HSE for other countries.

pipe exhausts that were needed for European models. New emissions regulations in California, which had often been out of step with the requirements of the other US states, also required a special 'California emissions package', which cost $100 extra on both the 4.0 SE and 4.6 HSE.

Although there was a slightly darker window tint than before, the main visual changes were to the colour and trim options. Four of the five new paint colours were at this stage exclusive to NAS models (*see* table later in this chapter), and two of them (AA Yellow and Monza Red) were described as having limited availability. Lightstone leather was added to the interior leather options for the 4.6 HSE only, and that model also gained a leather-trimmed gearshift grip. Meanwhile the 4.0 SE now came as standard with the Homelink system that had earlier been exclusive to the 4.6 HSE, and

WHAT THE PRESS THOUGHT

Generally speaking, the US motoring press had little new to say about the Range Rover in its later years. Initial impressions recorded in 1995–1996 remained valid in later summaries and buyers' guides.

This new Range Rover can hold its own with any luxury car in the vicinity of its $55,000 price.

[The more spacious interior is] a delight [and its ergonomics] a great leap forward.

[We] noticed no decline in the legendary off-road abilities, [but] some might wonder if this off-road expertise isn't overkill for what is basically a wealthy person's transport... [when]... only about one in six owners ever take their machines seriously off-road. Still, like a Porsche 911's 160mph top speed, the Range Rover's fabled off-road ability is part of its attraction, even if owners rarely take advantage of it.

[Performance is] modest... and top speed is only 113mph.
Car and Driver, April 1995

It may not be in the Range Rover's regal manner to drag race, but [the 4.0SE] needs more power behind the throne.

Highway handling is quite good... This is not a sports sedan, but you can hustle it down a curvy road with confidence.

We could easily live with the new Range Rover as our only family vehicle. In some respects, the earlier models have been

more entertainment than everyday vehicles. The new version is a better built machine with an interior that finally makes sense.
(*Road & Track*, May 1995)

Range Rovers are in a class of their own when it comes to sport-utility vehicles. And it's a class deserving of respect.

[The 4.6HSE] is more car-like than any Range Rover in history... The ride character would indicate independent suspension [and] there is a sense of agility on twisty roads that belies the size and upright nature of this sport-utility.

It's really difficult to drive one of these machines without feeling like the squire of the county.
(*Open Road*, December 1995)

Only serious motorheads will notice the big engine's not as smooth as the 4.0, because it's still ahead of the class. Although it is faster, the 4.6's big advantage is in driveability, where mid-range torque eliminates the need for a forced downshift.

The massive wheels on a 4.6 HSE don't lend themselves well to pavement use because there is little sidewall on the Pirelli Scorpions to protect them. That is also the reason you'll feel more road irregularities, but there's enough traction to go faster than any 2½ ton box has a right to go.
(*Road & Track Specials*, 1996)

there was a new option of an integrated hands-free cell-phone. This was mounted to the right of the radio and came with a roof-mounted antenna.

Later in the season, LRNA explored customer acceptance of higher-priced models with three limited editions. These were the Panther, the Kensington and the Vitesse. The Panther edition was not listed in LRNA's own guide to its Range Rover models, which suggests it may have been a regional rather than a national special edition.

Sales of the 1997 model-year Range Rover increased in Canada but went down in the USA. Nevertheless, the model was clearly very highly regarded. In May 1997 it was voted the best sport-utility vehicle on the market by readers of the *Robb Report*, the magazine considered to be the world's leading authority on the luxury lifestyle.

This was also the year when Range Rovers were used for the first time in the TReK competition, which pitted teams from Land Rover dealerships across the USA against one another in a test of teamwork, driving skill and physical and mental skills. The first of these competitions – which became annual – had been held in 1996, when the team vehicles had been Discoverys.

The 1997 NAS Limited Editions
Panther

As its name suggests, the Panther edition came in Beluga Black. It was based on a 4.6 HSE, and featured a number of enhancements from the new Autobiography options list. The Panther edition was released early in the 1997 calendar year; it is not clear how many were built, but a likely total is 250, although some commentators have suggested as many as 500.

Characteristics of the Panther edition were body-colour bumpers and a bright metal Panther-edition badge on each front wing. The interior had Lightstone leather with black piping, and a Panther logo was embroidered on the upper backrest panel of each front seat. There was an additional wood-trim package, and the Panther was the first NAS model to come with the 300-watt harmon/kardon premium ICE system that was planned for the 1998 model-year.

Kensington

The Kensington, named after West London's up-market dis-

One option on the 1997 Vitesse special edition was this eye-catching AA Yellow paint.

trict that contains shops such as Harrods, was again based on the 4.6 SE and cost $3,000 more than the standard model. There were 750 examples, in either Beluga Black or British Racing Green. Sales probably began around May 1997.

The upholstery was in Lightstone leather with Ash Black piping, and the leather trim was extended to the handbrake grip, the sides of the centre console, and the cubby box lid, which was also padded and hand stitched. Additional wood trim was complemented by a wooden cupholder inside the cubby box in place of the plastic type normally fitted to the underside of the lid. The Kensington edition also had the new 300-watt harmon/kardon ICE system.

Vitesse

Introduced at the same time as the Kensington edition, the Vitesse came in startling AA Yellow (already used on the NAS Defender 90) or bright Monza Red, in each case with Ash Black upholstery and chromed interior door releases. There was yellow seat piping with AA Yellow paint, and red piping with Monza Red. Otherwise this was a 1997-model 4.6 HSE with the new harmon/kardon ICE system, with the bib spoiler and door mirror heads painted to match the body, and the grille finished in black instead of the standard grey to give a stronger colour contrast with the body colour.

THE TREK RANGE ROVERS

LRNA's TReK event was primarily intended to foster team spirit and a greater understanding of the Land Rover ethos among dealer technicians. Created by LRNA's training unit, Land Rover University, it was first run in 1996, and became an annual competition for which North American dealerships were encouraged to put forward teams of three chosen from their own staff. The teams competed with one another in a variety of events focused on Land Rover vehicles, which tested teamwork, driving skill, and physical and mental skills.

A total of twenty 4.6 HSE Range Rovers were prepared for dealer teams competing in the 1997 event, which was held in Vermont during October. Their basic specification was that of the Vitesse limited edition, but they were actually 1998 models and had been prepared by LRSV. The whole front apron was painted yellow, as were the brush guards, and they had Futura wheels with yellow-painted centres. Each one carried a Safety Devices roofrack with rear ladder, yellow-painted lamp guards, a 9,000lb (4,080kg) Warn winch and under-chassis skid plates. The Range Rovers also carried multiple decals advertising the suppliers who supported the TReK event (notably BF Goodrich and Warn).

Although the TReK Range Rovers were not marketed as a special edition, most of them were sold on to the public after the event was over, still wearing their special livery and carrying their special equipment.

Prepare to be confused: although this is the 1997 TReK dealer team competition, it was held just as the 1998 models were becoming available – so this is a 1998 model, with its Futura wheels painted to match the rest of the vehicle.

Although LRNA's sales brochure for the Vitesse claimed that a total of 250 would be built, there were probably actually 350 of them (although a figure of 356 has also been quoted). The best sources suggest that 200 were in Monza Red and 150 in AA Yellow. Showroom price was $66,000 before extras.

The Vitesse name had been used during the 1980s to denote high-performance versions of Rover saloon cars, but these versions had never been sold in North America. Before that, it had belonged to the Triumph marque.

THE 1998 MODELS

There were two big items of news for North American Range Rover buyers at the start of the 1998 season in October 1997. The first was that the warranty had been extended to four years and 50,000 miles (or 80,000km in Canada); the second was that the 300-watt harmon/kardon audio system,

which had been previewed on 1997's limited-edition models, now came as standard on both the 4.0 SE and 4.6 HSE. This featured a head unit with AM, FM and Weatherband radio, plus a stereo cassette player and full electronic logic. The head unit also controlled a six-disc CD changer. The whole system played through twelve speakers, including a new sub-woofer.

Rather less exciting, although very noticeable to anybody who visited a Land Rover showroom, was that there were no individual model brochures for the new season; instead, there was a single all-model magazine, which LRNA promised to update every six months. Perhaps one reason for abandoning the single-model brochures was that there was not a lot new on the 1998-model Range Rovers, even though the 4.0 SE was distinguished by 16in Spyder alloy wheels on 255/65 tyres in place of its earlier Stratos type. There were several changes to the paint options as well, and a few interior changes completed the picture. The 1998-model 4.0 SE now had the same leather-trimmed gear-shift grip as the 4.6

A 1998-model 4.6 HSE, looking its best in Monza Red, with matching body-colour front apron and Mondial 18in alloy wheels.

The interior of a 1998 model shows the new six-pleat style of upholstery, which looked especially good with light colours such as this.

HSE, and both models gained the new six-pleat seat pattern, in every case with contrasting edge piping. Prices were now $56,000 for the 4.0 SE and $63,500 for the 4.6 HSE, both up by just $500 from their 1997 model-year levels.

As 1998 was the year of Land Rover's fiftieth anniversary, LRNA seized the opportunity to gain both extra publicity and extra sales by introducing a commemorative limited-edition Range Rover. This was introduced at the New York Auto Show in April 1998 – fifty years to the month since the Land Rover's first appearance at the Amsterdam Show. The 50th Anniversary Range Rover came with 18in Proline alloy wheels – the first 18in offering on a NAS 4.0-litre model.

For the 1998 model-year, sales climbed again in the USA – though not back to 1996 levels – and dipped slightly in Canada.

The 1998 US 50th Anniversary Limited Edition

Quite different from the UK 50th Anniversary edition, the North American one consisted of 275 Range Rovers based on the 4.0 SE. There were fifty examples for Canada and 225 for the USA. Each one was priced at $59,300 in the USA before extras were added – $3,300 above the cost of a standard 4.0 SE.

Unique to North America was this 50th Anniversary edition in Woodcote Green. This is a Canadian market example, with special decals on the rear wings, pictured at the Metro West dealership in Toronto, Canada, when brand new.

The 50th Anniversary models were based on 4.0 SE models.

There was a limited-edition plaque on the dashboard, too: Canada had fifty examples, of which this was number 5.

All 275 examples were painted Woodcote Green, with body-colour front apron and mirror heads, and Walnut leather upholstery with Lightstone seat piping, carpets and door trim. They had 255/55 tyres on Proline alloy wheels, which were an 18in style reserved for special editions at this stage. There were also special gold decal '50th Anniversary' logos on the rear bodysides and tailgate, and a brass plaque on the facia carried each vehicle's individual number within the limited edition. The US and Canadian editions were numbered separately.

THE 1999 MODELS

By the end of the 1998 model-year, LRNA still had quite large numbers of unsold 4.0-litre Range Rovers in the showrooms. So the company decided to delay the start of sales of the 1999 model-year vehicles with their new Thor V8 engines, and devised a strategy to dispose of the unsold vehicles.

The old-stock models were turned into two apparently new models. One was called the '4.0' and the other the '4.0 S'; in both cases, the appropriate letters were removed from their original '4.0 SE' tailgate badges, and in some cases a close look would show where this had been done. Both were then sold with a showroom price of $1,000 more than the 1998-model 4.0 SE. The justification for that extra $1,000 on the 4.0 model was a Land Rover Kit pack of accessories. On the 4.0 S, the $1,000 paid for a set of the 18in Mondial alloy wheels otherwise available only on the 4.6 HSE. Exactly how many unsold 1998 models received this treatment is not clear.

Meanwhile, a very special limited-edition 4.6-litre high-performance Range Rover had been developed in conjunction with the legendary US tuner Callaway Cars. Like the 4.0 and the 4.0 S, this was actually based on a 1998-specification model – although it had been planned some time in advance of its actual launch, and was specially built on the assembly lines at Solihull. It was also formidably expensive, at $75,000.

When the Thor-engined models did arrive, a couple of months into the new model-year, they brought with them further price increases. The entry-level 4.0 SE now cost $1,000 more than the 4.0 and the 4.0 S (so it was $2,000 more expensive than the 1998 4.0 SE), and the 4.6 HSE had gone up by $2,500 as compared to its 1998 equivalent. With the Thor engines also came twin-pipe exhaust systems and electronic traction control on all four wheels rather than

just on the rear axle. The new engines also brought different fuel consumption figures: the EPA 'City' figure for the 4.6-litre engine improved to 13mpg (21.8ltr/100km) from 1998's 12mpg (23.6ltr/100km), although the 'Highway' figure for the 4.0-litre dropped to 16mpg (17.7ltr/100km) from the previous year's 17mpg (16.6ltr/100km). (These were, of course, American gallons, which are smaller than the Imperial gallon measure used in the UK.)

There were some visual changes, too, as the 4.0 SE switched to Typhoon 16in alloy wheels, and the 4.6 HSE changed to 18in Hurricanes. New paint colours were only to be expected, while upholstery followed the changes for other markets as Walnut replaced Saddle as the brown option. Other interior changes included a new ICE head unit with RDS. There were also 'depowered' front airbags, front side airbags, and the seat belt pre-tensioners and load limiters seen on the 1999 Range Rovers for other markets. At a cost of $2,995, a factory-fitted in-dash satellite navigation system called JAMES could also be had. Showroom prices for the standard models were $58,525 for the 4.0 SE and $66,625 for the 4.6 HSE.

The 1999 season went on to become the best yet for Range Rover in North America, and failed to equal the previous year's total in Canada by just one vehicle.

The 1999 NAS Limited Editions

Callaway

The Callaway was a very special edition, created in the USA from late 1998-specification 4.6 HSE Range Rovers. There were 220 examples in three colours – Epsom Green, Niagara Grey and Rutland Red, the latter making a unique appearance on a North American Range Rover. Bumpers, grille, headlamp finishers and mirror heads were all in the body colour, and there was a Callaway decal on the tailgate; some probably had Callaway badges on the front wings as well. The wheels were Proline 18in alloys, and all the Callaway Range Rovers had Ash Black leather upholstery.

The base vehicle was a 4.6 HSE, which incorporated performance modifications by Callaway Cars in Old Lyme, Connecticut. In essence, the Callaway Range Rover combined lower gearing with a higher-revving and more powerful 4.6-litre engine to deliver the extra performance. Known to Callaway as the C11 project, the special-edition Range Rover was actually assembled at Solihull using special components shipped in from the USA. It was designed as a

Unique to North America was the Callaway edition. The engine was a reworked version of the standard 4.6-litre V8.

The Callaway edition had special tailgate badging and distinctive exhaust outlets.

The engine plenum cover also boasted of Callaway's involvement with this special edition.

carefully integrated package: many of the special Callaway items could not be fitted to other Range Rovers, and standard Range Rover equivalents could not be used as service replacements.

The key changes were in the drivetrain. Cylinder-head work raised the compression ratio to 9.60:1, adding reshaped ports, tapered valve guides and unique valve seat geometry. A special air intake also raised the air-flow rate, while exhaust back-pressure was reduced by a special centre silencer. The injection plenum carried the Callaway name, and the GEMS control system was modified to suit.

The Callaway engine developed 240bhp at 5,000rpm and 285lb/ft at 3,500rpm, and drove through a special torque converter and modified transfer gearbox with lowered gearing of 1.294:1 in high range and 3.481:1 in low range. (These transfer boxes were identified by a red serial number plate.) The front axle was uprated with stronger drive shafts and a four-pin differential to take the extra input. A Callaway Range Rover was claimed to accelerate from 0–60mph in 8.6sec, as compared to 9.7sec for a standard NAS 4.6-litre HSE.

The interior had extra wood trim on the facia and centre console, and many examples of the Callaway were fitted with a GPS system. The facia carried a numbered limited-edition plaque, the gearshift knob had the Callaway logo embossed into its leather covering, and the lid of the centre cubby was upholstered in leather over the plastic of the standard moulding.

Canadian Autobiography

Even though the Autobiography scheme had its effect on US limited editions in this period, there were no Autobiography editions as such for the USA. However, it appears that there was a 4.6 HSE Autobiography edition for Canada during the 1999 model-year. Few details are available, and quantities are not known, but these special-edition models had Autobiography extended wood packages (with extra wood on the dash, centre console, shift grip and handbrake lever) and seat piping to match the exterior colour. They carried Autobiography script logos inside on the centre console and on the tailgate next to the 4.6 HSE badge.

Dealer Limited Editions

Some North American dealers created their own 'limited editions' to stimulate sales. Among these was the Black Tie edition, a 1999 model in Java Black with either Ash Black or Granite Grey upholstery. It appears to have been confined to a dealer or dealers in the Florida region, and carried a distinctive white decal showing a top hat and cane.

THE 2000 MODELS

For the 2000 model-year, LRNA adopted the same strategy as they had in the previous one, selling the last of the 1999 models at the start of the season with lower prices and special names, and then bringing in the 'real' 2000 models later with higher prices. The early models did not have the clear and smoked lamp lenses, 'round' headlamp masks, body-coloured front apron or bright tailgate release button of the later ones.

As in the previous year, there were two varieties of 'early' 4.0-litre Range Rover. The entry-level model was called the Range Rover County, and cost $300 more than the 1999 4.0 SE. It was available in only three colours – Kent

Green, Java Black or White Gold – in each case with the Lightstone leather interior normally associated with the 4.6 HSE, and with the latest Lightning 16in alloy wheels. For an extra $700, buyers could have the Range Rover 4.0, which had a Land Rover Kit pack of a brush bar, roofrack and lamp guards.

There were also two 'early' 4.6-litre models over the late summer of 1999, known as the 4.6 HSK and Vitesse. The Vitesse was marketed as a limited edition and is discussed separately; the 4.6 HSK was distinguished by additional interior wood trim and by a hands-free cellphone. It cost $1,000 more than the 1999 4.6 HSE.

The 'proper' 2000 models were announced in late September 1999, and wore familiar badging as the 4.0 SE and 4.6 HSE models; prices were $59,000 and $67,300 respectively. They were followed by a special limited edition called the 4.6 Vitesse. The 4.0 SE had Lightning alloy wheels like the 'early' 2000 4.0-litre models, while the 4.6 HSE continued with the 18in Hurricane style. LRNA boasted that both sizes of the Thor V8 now met the Californian Low Emissions Vehicle (LEV) standards, which were tighter than those in the other US states. To do this, they had a secondary air injection pump and a modified catalytic converter. Other details on the 2000 models were electro-chromic door mirrors and green instrument lighting, as seen on 2000-model Range Rovers for other markets.

There were, of course, some limited editions. The County and 4.0 models sold at the start of the model-year were not strictly limited editions, and nor was the 4.6 HSK, so the first of the 2000 special editions was the Vitesse. There was then a group of four limited editions that were previewed at the New York Auto Show, which opened on 20 April 2000. Three of them were North American versions of 'global' limited editions – the Holland & Holland, the Linley and the 30th Anniversary (*see* Chapter 4) – but unique to North America was the 4.6 HSE Rhino. Examples of the 30th Anniversary edition did not in fact become available until the start of the 2001 model-year.

LRNA had expected sales to begin falling in the 2000 model-year, estimating that 7,200 Range Rovers would find customers as against 7,389 the previous season. In fact the drop was greater than the company anticipated, and actual sales in the USA were just 6,957.

The 2000 NAS Limited Editions

Vitesse (1999)

Based on the 4.6 HSE, this was a 250-strong limited edition in Java Black with a body-colour grille, additional wood trim, and a satellite navigation system as standard. The interior was finished in Walnut.

Linley (April 2000)

Although the Range Rover Linley was offered in the USA, it was only ever built to special order. The list price was $125,000. Just one example was sold there, reportedly to a dotcom millionaire who paid in cash!

Holland & Holland (April 2000)

There were 125 Holland & Holland Range Rovers for the USA. Their specification was unchanged from the UK examples (see above), although of course they had left-hand drive. These were priced at $79,000.

Rhino (April 2000)

The 125-strong Rhino edition was based on a 4.6 HSE painted in Bonatti Grey (which would be a 2001 colour) with body-colour bumpers, sills and mirror heads. Hurricane alloy wheels were standard, with a wrap-around brush bar. Special dark grey rhino-skin effect textured leather was used for the pleated sections of the seats, and for other leather-trimmed items in the cabin. The wood trim was in greenish-grey Poplar Anthracite, and a JAMES satellite navigation system was standard.

Each example carried a bright metal rhino logo on the tailgate and front wings, and owners were presented with a small wooden rhino memento, which had been carved in Africa. The base cost of the Rhino edition was $77,000.

THE 2001 MODELS

The 2001 Range Rovers brought with them the final major change in the NAS model line-up. The 4.0-litre models were dropped altogether, and the 4.6-litre engine became the only one available. There were two variants: a 4.6 SE in place of the old 4.0 SE, and a 4.6 HSE as before. Both of them now came with a slightly larger fuel tank, holding 24.6 US gallons (93ltr), and in Canada, all 2001 models came with child seat tether anchors.

There were clear visual distinctions between the two models. The SE had 16in Lightning wheels with 255/65 tyres, and the HSE had 18in Hurricane alloys with 255/55 tyres. The HSE also had a bright metal highlight in its side bump-strips. Before extras, the SE cost $62,625 and the HSE $68,625, in each case inclusive of the $625 'destination charge'.

There were also differences between the two models

The Rhino edition for 2000 previewed the new Bonatti Grey paint. Production examples carried small rhino-shaped badges, but this publicity picture does not show them.

Grey wood trim was teamed with specially textured upholstery in the Rhino edition.

inside the passenger cabin. The HSE came with a 460-watt harmon/kardon ICE system featuring digital sound processing (DSP), and a newly redesigned satellite navigation system as standard. The model also had new woodgrain trim panels on the upper centre console, window-switch surround and rear ash-tray panels. Its cubby box and centre console sides were finished in leather to match the seating surfaces. Standard on the SE was the older 300-watt system, with

THE GREAT DIVIDE 10TH ANNIVERSARY EVENT

In 1989, Land Rover had introduced the 1990-model Range Rovers to the press on an event called the Great Divide Expedition. Billed as the first north-south off-road crossing of the Continental Divide by motor vehicle, in this expedition a group of specially prepared Range Rovers threaded their way along the line of the US Continental Divide between Denver and Colorado, for the most part high up in the mountains on National Forest roads.

In October 1999, LRNA ran a '10th Anniversary' event, to gain publicity for the Range Rover. Journalists were invited to join specific stages of the trip, which encompassed some especially challenging driving amid spectacular scenery. The 1999 trip was run between Telluride and Denver, and lasted for four days, with between nine and ten hours' driving on each day. Interestingly, the vehicles used on the trip were 1999 models; presumably, examples of the forthcoming 2000-model Range Rovers were not available in time.

In 2014, Land Rover would run a 25th Anniversary event, once again as a way of publicising the latest Range Rovers.

The event vehicles all carried this special decal logo. NICK DIMBLEBY

ABOVE: **A typical scene in Colorado during the 1999 Great Divide Expedition.** NICK DIMBLEBY

The Great Divide Expedition 10th Anniversary event was held in 1999, with 1999-model vehicles rather than the new 2000 models that would soon become available. NICK DIMBLEBY

For 2001, a new 4.6 SE was created as the entry-level model.

no satellite navigation. However, the satnav and 460-watt ICE could be specified as an upgrade for the SE at a cost of $2,995, when the additional woodgrain trim and leather trim enhancements were included as part of the package.

The HSE could also be ordered with options. When Lightstone upholstery was among them, this could be accompanied by carpets and seat piping to match the exterior colour (but only on four of the colour options) for an extra $750. It was also possible to order a wood-and-leather steering wheel, which cost a further $400.

NAS Range Rover sales in the 2001 model-year were supported by only one special edition, which was the 30th Anniversary model that had been announced at the New York Show in April 2000. Perhaps LRNA saw no reason to put the extra effort into pushing sales, which for 2001 slid quite

dramatically to just 4,856 in the USA. The new Range Rover was, of course, just a few months away from its introduction, and expectations were high, no doubt deterring some potential buyers of the 38A models. Paradoxically, sales in Canada increased during 2001, and were up to 205 from the 2000-season total of 142.

The 2001 US 30th Anniversary Limited Edition

The USA took 200 of the 30th Anniversary edition that was also built for Japan, Switzerland and the UK (*see* Chapter 4). Although announced at the New York Show in April 2000, it did not actually go on sale until September 2000. The cost was around $71,000.

ABOVE: **The 2002 4.6 HSE retained its appeal to the end, when it was replaced by the new L322 model.**

The 2002 NAS Range Rover remained a model of luxurious discretion. This one is fitted with the JAMES satellite navigation system, which occupied the same space on the centre console as the CARiN system used on European models.

THE 2002 MODELS

LRNA began the promotional build-up to the new third-generation Range Rover in the autumn of 2001, announcing it to the North American public at the Detroit Motor Show in January 2002, although actual sales were not scheduled to begin until July. So it was quite a challenge to keep interest alive in the existing 38A range throughout the long anticipatory period. As 38A production ended in December 2001, all the LRNA stock for the 2002 model-year was built in the last months of that year.

No major new features were forthcoming from Solihull, and for 2002 the North American line-up was reduced to a single model – the 4.6 HSE. There was only one new paint colour for the mainstream models, too. LRNA added a few minor changes to the specification, but essentially had to rely on injections of interest from three limited editions. However, this did not leave the company short-changed for 2002, because the Land Rover Freelander was launched into the USA that year, and generated its own new volumes of showroom traffic and sales.

Meanwhile, all the NAS 38As for 2002 now came with heated seats for both driver and front passenger, 18in Hurricane alloy wheels, and deep tinted 'privacy' glass from the B-pillar backwards as standard. Also standard was the 460-watt harmon-kardon ICE system with DSP technology including speed equalization, and of course the associated GPS system that incorporated off-road navigation.

The three limited editions were called the Borrego, the Westminster and the Rhino – the latter tying in with LRNA's 2002 sponsorship of the Rhino Compound at the Fossil Rim Wildlife Centre in Glen Rose, Texas. The Rhino edition was treated as an end-of-line edition by LRNA. Yet the interest that these special editions created was not enough to prevent 38A Range Rover sales sliding down to a paltry 3,927 units in the USA.

The 2002 US Limited Editions

Borrego (2002)

The Borrego was a 100-strong limited edition based on the 4.6 HSE. It was named after its eye-catching Borrego Yellow paint (not available on any other Range Rover), and came with Ash Black Oxford leather upholstery that featured yellow stitching. The interior also featured chrome for the shift knob, the handbrake and for the door casing accents. The

wheels were 18in Comet alloys. These models had a showroom price of $72,665.

Westminster (2002)

The Westminster was a 250-strong limited edition based on the 4.6 HSE. It had Java Black paint with colour-matched bumpers and sills, plus Proline 18in alloy wheels. The interior was in Ash Black Oxford leather, but with Piano Black wood trim, plus chrome bezels and mouldings. This edition was priced slightly higher than the contemporary Borrego.

Rhino (2002)

The Rhino was a 100-strong 'final' edition in Bonatti Grey, with the special Rhino-textured leather upholstery that had been seen on the 2000 Rhino edition. The 2002 version again had Poplar Anthracite wood trim, with chrome on the interior door handles and around the instrument dials. However, a distinguishing feature was that these 'final' NAS models had Proline 18in alloy wheels rather than the Hurricane wheels of the earlier Rhino edition.

NORTH AMERICAN RANGE ROVER SALES

The best year for sales of first-generation Range Rovers in the USA was 1995, when 5,655 examples were sold. The best year in Canada was 1993, when 158 were sold.

For the second-generation models, the best year in the USA was 1999 (7,389 examples) and the best year in Canada was 1997 (306 examples).

	USA	Canada
1995	2,975	109
1996	7,000	248
1997	6,673	306
1998	6,826	278
1999	7,389	277
2000	6,957	142
2001	4,856	205
2002	3,927	64
Totals	**46,603**	**1,629**

PAINT AND TRIM COMBINATIONS FOR NORTH AMERICAN RANGE ROVERS

The 1995 Model-Year

For the 1995 model-year there were eight exterior colours available, in each case with just one interior colour option. All these colours were also available for other countries. All interiors were in Saddle leather except with Aspen Silver, when Granite leather was used. Beluga Black paint was an extra-cost option.

The Combinations Available

Paint	Upholstery	Paint	Upholstery
Alpine White	Saddle	Biarritz Blue	Saddle
Aspen Silver	Granite	Epsom Green	Saddle
Avalon Blue	Saddle	Portofino Red	Saddle
Beluga Black	Saddle	Roman Bronze	Saddle

The 1996 Model-Year

For the 1996 model-year there were eight exterior colours, of which four were new. Five of these colours were available only on the 4.0 SE, one was exclusive to the 4.6 HSE, and two could be ordered on both models.

There were three interior colours, but each was tied to certain colours, and there were no options. Ash Black upholstery was unique to the 4.6 HSE.

The Combinations Available

	Upholstery colour	Model availability
Alpine White	Saddle	4.0 SE, 4.6 HSE
Altai Silver	Granite	4.0 SE
Avalon Blue	Saddle	4.0 SE
Beluga Black	Saddle	4.0 SE
	Ash Black	4.6 HSE
Epsom Green	Saddle	4.0 SE
Niagara Grey	Granite	4.0 SE
Rioja Red	Saddle	4.6 HSE
Willow Green	Saddle	4.0 SE

The 1997 Model-Year

For the 1997 model-year there were eleven exterior colours, of which five were new. Four of these colours were unique to NAS models at this stage: AA Yellow, British Racing Green, Monza Red and White Gold.

The 4.0 SE was available in eight colours, and the 4.6 HSE in six; three colours were available on both models. Beluga Black cost extra on the 4.0 SE, and AA Yellow and Monza Red cost extra on the 4.6 HSE.

There were four interior colours; Granite and Saddle were available only for the 4.0 SE, and Ash Black and Lightstone only for the 4.6 HSE.

The Combinations Available

	Upholstery	Model
AA Yellow	Ash Black	4.6 HSE
Alpine White	Saddle	4.0 SE
	Lightstone	4.6 HSE
Altai Silver	Granite	4.0 SE
Beluga Black	Saddle	4.0 SE
	Lightstone	4.6 HSE
	Ash Black	4.6 HSE
British Racing Green	Lightstone	4.6 HSE
Epsom Green	Saddle	4.0 SE
Monza Red	Lightstone	4.6 HSE
Oxford Blue	Saddle	4.0 SE
Rioja Red	Saddle	4.0 SE
	Lightstone	4.6 HSE
White Gold	Saddle	4.0 SE
Willow Green	Saddle	4.0 SE

The 1998 Model-Year

For the 1998 model-year there were nine exterior colours, of which two were new. Seven of these colours were available on the 4.0 SE and five on the 4.6 HSE (of which two were unique to the model). Outside North America, British Racing Green was available only through the Autobiography programme. Beluga Black was an extra-cost option on the 4.0 SE.

There were again four interior colours. Ash Black and Saddle remained the 4.0 SE options, while Ash Black and Lightstone were unique to the 4.6 HSE.

The Combinations Available

	Upholstery	Model
Altai Silver	Granite	4.0 SE
Beluga Black	Saddle	4.0 SE
	Lightstone or Ash Black	4.6 HSE
British Racing Green	Lightstone	4.6 HSE
Chawton White	Saddle	4.0 SE
	Lightstone or Ash Black	4.6 HSE
Epsom Green	Saddle	4.0 SE
Oxford Blue	Saddle	4.0 SE
	Lightstone	4.6 HSE
Rioja Red	Saddle	4.0 SE
White Gold	Lightstone	4.6 HSE
Woodcote Green	Saddle	4.0 SE

PAINT AND TRIM COMBINATIONS FOR NORTH AMERICAN RANGE ROVERS (*continued*)

The 1999 Model-Year

For the 1999 model-year there were eight exterior colours, of which four were new. As usual, one colour was unique to the 4.6 HSE, and this year just one was unique to the 4.0 SE.

There were four interior colours; for the 4.0 SE the primary colour was Walnut (replacing last year's Saddle), but Granite was specified with Blenheim Silver paint. Ash Black and Lightstone upholstery were unique to the 4.6 HSE.

The 4.0 and 4.0 S models sold early in the 1999 model-year had paint and trim combinations from the 1998 model-year options list. The Callaway limited edition was available in Epsom Green, Niagara Grey and (uniquely for North America) Rutland Red.

The Combinations Available

	Upholstery	Model
Blenheim Silver	Granite	4.0 SE
	Ash Black	4.6 HSE
Chawton White	Walnut	4.0 SE
	Ash Black or Lightstone	4.6 HSE
Epsom Green	Ash Black	4.6 HSE, Callaway
	Lightstone	4.6 HSE
Java Black	Walnut	4.0 SE
	Ash Black or Lightstone	4.6 HSE
Niagara Grey	Ash Black	4.6 HSE, Callaway
	Lightstone	4.6 HSE
Oxford Blue	Walnut	4.0 SE
	Ash Black or Lightstone	4.6 HSE
Rioja Red	Walnut	4.0 SE
Rutland Red	Ash Black	Callaway
White Gold	Walnut	4.0 SE
	Ash Black or Lightstone	4.6 HSE

The 2000 Model-Year

For the 2000 model-year there were nine exterior colours, of which two (Alveston Red and Kent Green) were new; Rioja Red had been dropped. White Gold was available in limited volumes only.

The paint and trim combinations were simplified this year. Both the 4.6 SE and the 4.6 HSE were available in the full range of paint colours, but Java Black was an extra-cost option for the 4.6 SE. There were two interior colour options for every exterior colour. On the 4.6 SE, these were Granite Grey and Walnut; on the 4.6 HSE they were Ash Black and Lightstone.

The Paint Colours Available

Alveston Red	Epsom Green	Niagara Grey
Blenheim Silver	Java Black	Oxford Blue
Chawton White	Kent Green	White Gold

The 2001 Model-Year

Once again there were nine paint colours for the 2001 model-year. Bonatti Grey replaced Niagara Grey and Oslo Blue replaced Oxford Blue. In the USA, Java Black was again available on the SE only at extra cost, but it was a no-cost option in Canada.

Granite Grey and Walnut upholstery were available with all exterior colours on the 4.6 SE. For the 4.6 HSE, Granite Grey, Walnut, Ash Black and Lightstone were available with all exterior colours. Lightstone leather with contrasting carpets and seat piping was available only as indicated in the table below, at extra cost in the USA but cost free in Canada.

The Paint Colours Available

	Lightstone contrast colour		Lightstone contrast colour
Alveston Red	Olde Red	Java Black	N/A
Blenheim Silver	N/A	Kent Green	Classic Green
Bonatti Grey	N/A	Oslo Blue	Prussian Blue
Chawton White	N/A	White Gold	N/A
Epsom Green	Classic Green		

The 2002 Model-Year

For the 2002 model-year there were nine 'standard' exterior colours, the only difference from 2001 being that Vienna Green had replaced Kent Green. In addition, Borrego Yellow was available on the Borrego limited edition.

As in 2001, Granite Grey, Walnut, Ash Black and Lightstone were available with all exterior colours. Lightstone leather with contrasting carpets and seat piping was available only as indicated in the table below.

The Paint Colours Available

	Lightstone contrast colour		Lightstone contrast colour
Alveston Red	Olde Red	Java Black	N/A
Blenheim Silver	N/A	Oslo Blue	Prussian Blue
Bonatti Grey	N/A	Vienna Green	Classic Green
Chawton White	N/A	White Gold	N/A
Epsom Green	Classic Green		

AUTOBIOGRAPHY

Autobiography was Land Rover's custom-finishing pro-gramme. It had been introduced for the first-generation Range Rover at the London Motorfair in October 1993, but it was not until after the introduction of the 38A model that Land Rover realized its full potential.

Ever since the late 1950s, Land Rover had operated a custom-finishing department of sorts, but in the beginning its focus had been on special adaptations of the utility mod-els for commercial purposes. Known initially as the Special Projects Department, its primary business was to examine aftermarket conversions and decide whether they would compromise the integrity of the basic factory-built vehi-cle. Conversions that complied were granted 'Land Rover Approval', which meant that they would retain the standard factory warranty, could be ordered through Land Rover dealers rather than direct from the converter, and would be promoted by Land Rover itself as well. There were obvi-ous benefits to the aftermarket specialists, and the scheme worked well for many years.

Most Autobiography models carried an underbonnet plaque with the contract number on it. This one was on a 1999 model.

After 1970, the Special Projects Department turned its attention to aftermarket conversions for the Range Rover as well as the utility Land Rovers. However, Land Rover rather misjudged the market for Range Rover conversions in the 1970s, focusing its efforts on such things as ambulances and fire tenders, when the growing market was for better performance and greater luxury. In 1985, Special Projects was renamed as Special Vehicle Operations, and by the end of the decade Land Rover had determined to reorganize its SVO division with the aim of bringing back in-house as much as possible of the conversions business – both for Range Rovers and for Land Rovers – in order to maximize profits.

The reorganization was complete by 1992, when SVO was renamed Land Rover Special Vehicles (LRSV). One of the most noticeable changes was the introduction of the Autobiography programme the following year, and it is said that its inception was helped by the availability of a number of skilled coachbuilders and craftsmen who had been made redundant when Jaguar had stopped making the Daimler DS420 Vanden Plas limousine in 1992.

As far as the customers were concerned, Autobiogra-phy was a bespoke finishing service for Range Rovers that allowed them to specify their own choice of paint and uphol-stery colours, plus whatever combination of features from the options list that they wanted. The scheme was marketed as 'the ultimate personalization'. Within Land Rover, how-ever, its horizons were much broader. The idea was that the system would also be used to develop a range of new fea-tures that could be used as a menu from which special- and limited-edition models could be easily created. If customer acceptance of these new features was good, they could then be transferred to the mainstream models.

Autobiography worked by taking part-built vehicles from the main assembly lines and then adding the bespoke fea-tures in the LRSV workshops (or, in a few cases, with the assistance of outside contractors). By the time of the 38A Range Rover, it was standard practice to use black vehicles as the basis of those that were to have an exterior colour change. This avoided the need to remove the engine to repaint the engine bay, as a black engine bay was considered to be acceptable with any exterior colour. However, in cases where the Autobiography system was used to produce small-run limited editions, the bodyshells were painted in the intended colour from the beginning and the vehicles did not therefore have black engine bays.

INTRODUCING THE PROGRAMME

It took LRSV some time to work up a menu of options for the 38A models, not least because this menu was partly shaped by customer feedback as the first of the new Range Rovers reached their owners. So although the 38A had been introduced in autumn 1994, it was autumn 1996 before the Autobiography programme for these models was announced at the 1996 Motor Show. Even then, it was more of a statement of intent than anything else, because in practice the first Autobiography models were not available until the following summer. In October 1996 the press release claimed:

The Autobiography service allows the customer to choose from more than half a million permutations to create a totally unique vehicle to suit his or her individual taste. Most visual of these is the choice of non-standard exterior colours, which can be extended to include colour-coordinated bumpers, door mirrors and spoilers.

The Autobiography interior may be specified with a choice of leather seat colours and styles, including traditional and modern stitch patterns and extensive use of burr walnut to the switch panel, cubby box lid, handbrake lever, rear ashtray and rear vent. Colour-keyed lambswool rugs to front and rear, and smoked glass in a choice of tints, are available.

In addition, the scheme allowed customers to order a VHS video player mounted in the centre console and which played through screens mounted in the back of the front-seat headrests. Sound was conveyed through infra-red headphones. From spring 1997 it would also be possible to order a Philips CARiN satellite navigation system.

Not surprisingly, the demonstrator Autobiography Range Rover on the 1996 show stand highlighted all these features.

This picture was used to illustrate the Autobiography scheme on its announcement in October 1996. The paint was special, and so was the colour-coding of bumpers and mirror bodies. The Triple Sport wheels were unique to LRSV at the time.

An early Autobiography interior, distinguished by two-tone leather and additional wood trim on the cubby box and gear selector lever. NICK DIMBLEBY

Early Autobiography models had a decal script badge on the tailgate. NICK DIMBLEBY

LEFT: **This left-hand-drive Autobiography Range Rover shows one of the more common wood options.**

Based on a 4.6 HSE – as all Autobiography models would be – it had non-standard Ascot Green paint with body-colour bumpers, front spoiler, sills and door mirror heads. It also had medium-tinted glass, and introduced a new alloy wheel design called Triple Sport, which would only ever be available through Land Rover Parts as an accessory fit – or, of course, through the Autobiography programme.

The interior showcased all the planned options. The basic interior colour was Lightstone, but the wearing surfaces of the seats were in contrasting Lichen leather. The seats were piped in Wild Green, and there were Arden Green lambswool over-rugs front and rear. Additional burr walnut wood trim was fitted to the instrument binnacle, facia, gearshift surround, centre console and dash console, and there were matching picnic tables on the backs of the front seats. The price was announced as £61,190.43 – over £15,000, or 30 per cent, more than the cost of a 4.6 HSE – and the CARiN navigation system was promised at extra cost for later.

The first Autobiography 38A Range Rovers were probably built for individual customers in late 1996 or early 1997, but as these were special orders they were not publicized. So the next time the Autobiography name attracted public attention was in summer 1997, when it was applied to a special edition for the UK market. As promised earlier, this showcased the CARiN satellite navigation system. Part of its purpose was to enable Land Rover to gauge how many customers were prepared to pay such a high price for a Range Rover.

EXPERIMENTAL CONCEPTS

In this early period, LRSV looked at developing its Autobiography programme in a number of ways. As a result, the division built a small number of experimental or concept vehicles that were then evaluated as possibilities for future production. Three of these are known: a six-door limousine, a Sports Concept and a Mobile Office Concept.

The Limousine Prototype

Although the Middle East market for custom conversions of the Range Rover was declining by the mid-1990s, Land

A six-door limousine prototype was built as the Autobiography programme
was getting into its stride. However, it remained unique.

The six-door model offered luxurious seating for six, or could take eight if necessary. Note the Autobiography badge on the tailgate.

Rover was determined to be ready and waiting with options for the new model if the market picked up again. In practice, that did not happen, which was certainly one reason why the six-door limousine remained a unique vehicle.

LRSV managed to secure a redundant factory demonstrator as the basis of their prototype, a 1996-model 4.0-litre SE (with VIN SALLPAMJ3TA-338623), which had supposedly been an Australian-specification showcase. It had probably already been registered as N788 ARW by this stage. The vehicle was essentially cut in half and put back together with a new centre section containing an extra row of seats that were accessed through an additional pair of doors. The new

second-row doors were made up using adapted production parts, and LRSV manager Rob Myers remembered that a good deal of juggling was required during assembly to get them to line up satisfactorily. The problem was that the swage lines on the body sides rise slightly towards the rear of the vehicle, and so in the standard panel they were not in quite the right place.

Needless to say, the original 4.0-litre engine was swapped for a 4.6-litre V8 to deal more effectively with the additional weight of the long-wheelbase conversion. The modified vehicle was completed in time to be displayed at a motor show in the Middle East, with the intention of promoting the idea of bespoke custom conversions among likely customers. However, there was no call for any copies of the Autobiography limousine, and the vehicle was quickly sidelined at Land Rover.

Nevertheless, there was a residual interest in it. News of its existence filtered out to film and television companies, and as a result it played a minor role as the chauffeur-driven transport for M (Judi Dench), the head of the Secret Service in the James Bond film *The World Is Not Enough*. For that role, the centre row of seats was reversed to face backwards so that M and Bond could be filmed facing one another during a discussion.

The six-door prototype was also lent to a few celebrities for major events, a notable one being singer Elton John's birthday party; however, by 2000 it was scheduled to be scrapped as redundant. It was saved from that fate by the Dunsfold Collection of Land Rovers, which now takes care of it.

The Sports Concept

Very little information is available about the Sports Concept vehicle, which was supposedly displayed on the Land Rover stand at the 1998 NEC Motor Show; however, it did not figure in the official show catalogue. Based on a 4.6-litre model, the car was painted in Deep Windsor Pearl and had body-coloured Pro-Sport alloy wheels. Its interior featured Ash leather with suede and Light Granite piping, a CARiN satellite navigation system, and a television screen in each front headrest.

The Mobile Office

One of the options that LRSV was keen to investigate was to turn the Range Rover into a mobile office for the business executive who typically spent a lot of time in transit

P880 KAC became the prototype Mobile Office, but was too expensive to put into production.

The Mobile Office featured a control panel concealed within the cubby box ...

LEFT: **... and a laptop computer on the back seat.**

These were early days for mobile communications technology, and this cabinet containing the electronic circuitry took up much of the loadspace.

between one office and another. The Mobile Office Concept was developed in conjunction with Unique Technic, the mobile communications company owned by television personality (and Range Rover enthusiast) Noel Edmonds. LRSV had been looking at the idea of a Range Rover Mobile Office since at least 1992, when they had built one from a long-wheelbase Vogue LSE, and this latest venture was a continuation of their original line of thinking.

Although mobile communications have since become a fact of everyday life, in 1997 the technology was still in its early stages (the first Apple iPhone was not released until 2007). As a result, much of the equipment used in the concept vehicle now looks clunky and old-fashioned – but it was cutting-edge technology for the time, and was expensive, too: the claimed development cost of this vehicle was an eye-watering £450,000.

The host vehicle, with VIN SALLPAMJ3VA-354047, started life as a black 4.6 HSE in October 1996, and probably went straight to LRSV for the Autobiography programme. LRSV registered it on 18 March 1997, by which time it had probably been painted in special Ming Blue, trimmed in cream Cheshire-grade leather with a wood-and-leather steering wheel, and given the Triple Sport wheels, which at this stage were unique to Special Vehicles. The date is early enough for this to have been an early trials vehicle for the Autobiography custom-finishing process.

At some time between then and mid-1998, the vehicle was kitted out by Unique Technic. As this was very much a pioneering scheme, the Range Rover was fitted with all kinds of technology, and was a showcase for the possible rather than the strictly necessary. Anticipating big electrical loads, LRSV fitted a police-specification 120-amp alternator, a big-capacity diesel-spec battery, and a second battery in the rear. A police-spec screened ignition system and BeCM were also added to avoid likely problems with interference.

As telephone communications were obviously a high priority, there were phones front and rear. Equally obviously, a laptop computer was needed, and that had its own docking station attached to the back of the left-hand rear seat. That seat was folded down when the 'office' was in use. Behind the laptop sat a colour printer, and there was also entertainment available for the rear-seat passenger from an 'ordinary' Autobiography VHS video-tape player in an extended centre console, with a pair of television screens in the back of the headrests.

Microphone pick-ups and concealed cameras around the cabin allowed whatever was said or done inside the vehicle to be picked up and recorded. The system could be used for video conferencing, because it was linked to a video transmission unit that operated through a GSM satellite phone link, but it also had an anti-theft function. As a rather pleased Noel Edmonds put it when the Range Rover was displayed

The Mobile Office that became available through the Autobiography programme in 1999 was much simpler, with an extended centre console and a split rear seat. Equipment included a PC with infra-red keyboard and an LCD VDU screen in the front seat back. A fax machine was optional.

at the London computer trade show Comdex in October 1998, 'If the car is stolen, it phones to let you know. It even shows you a picture of the … who's nicked it!' In a worst case scenario, for the businessman under attack, a panic button would send out images through the Cellnet digital network to a monitoring station.

By the time of that trade show, Edmonds seems to have been using it as his own mobile office, and was expected to cover 50,000 miles (80,500km) a year in it. The vehicle was displayed on the stand of mobile communications specialists Cellnet, and would later do stints as a demonstrator for Land Rover, and also for Sony, who contributed some of its on-board equipment.

However, the concept went no further. Land Rover's owners at BMW had already vetoed expensive upgrades for the second-generation Range Rover, preferring to put the cash into developing the all-new third-generation model. So LRSV were probably instructed to take the project no further, and for the 1999 model-year an altogether simpler Mobile Office conversion became available from LRSV. Noel Edmonds sold on the Unique vehicle later that year, and it still survives at the time of writing, with all of its on-board equipment still intact but some of it no longer functional.

THE AUTOBIOGRAPHY STRATEGY

Against a background of minimum change on the mainstream models for 1998, Land Rover planned a new strategy for Autobiography and limited-edition variants of the Range Rover. The stated aim behind these was to generate press and customer interest, and to enhance the aspirational nature of the Range Rover; at the same time, limited editions using selected Autobiography options were to be used to explore the upper limits of Range Rover market positioning. The marketing team had also come up with the concept of a 'halo' limited edition that would unite all the Autobiography options then on offer, and announced its plan to produce one in the first quarter of every calendar year, starting with 1998.

At the start of the 1998 season, a new Autobiography tailgate badge was introduced. Where the original had been a decal, the new one was cast from solid metal. As an option, it could be had in 18-carat gold instead. The Autobiography programme was now promoted as offering twenty-five special colours that were not available on showroom models,

For 1998, the Autobiography badge was cast from metal. A solid gold one became available, too – at a price. NICK DIMBLEBY

and these were colours that the LRSV team had selected as suitable for the Range Rover. None of that, of course, prevented a customer from ordering a colour that was on neither list.

As for interiors, promotional literature claimed that the Autobiography programme offered a choice of 300,000 Cheshire leather finishes; many of these featured a colour contrast between the bolsters and the pleated sections of the seats. There was an 'unlimited' choice of wood finishes, and of course carpets and overmats would be provided to tone in with whatever colours the customer had chosen for the upholstery. Most important to those who were paying money for these features was perhaps the knowledge that each Autobiography Range Rover took over 100 hours of hand craftsmanship to finish.

This 1998 Autobiography has a special metallic custom paint called Iris, and initially served as a show car and demonstrator. The Hurricane wheels in this picture are not the style originally fitted.

At the same time, LRSV started looking at how the Autobiography programme could be better promoted overseas. So in the first half of 1999, they experimented with a 'generic' Autobiography edition in Japan, by sending out kits of parts that could be incorporated into fully built vehicles that were already in showrooms. The parts included a full wood kit and interior chrome package, plus a full set of seat covers to permit a retrim, with a leather enhancement pack for the door pulls, glove box and knee bolster in a contrasting colour. As a second experiment, they planned a series of Autobiography 'studios' in selected places overseas, where customers could go to choose the options to make up their own individual Range Rover specification. The first of these was in Kuwait, which had opened for business by September 1999.

It is not possible at present to say how many Autobiography Range Rovers were built during the production run of the 38A. However, internal documents show that the target for 1998 was 2,600 vehicles, and that the target for 1999 was 2,000 vehicles. Whether these targets were met is not clear.

TOP LEFT: **A VHS video tape player was available from the Autobiography programme, and fitted into an extended centre console.** NICK DIMBLEBY

TOP RIGHT: **The video tape player was linked to a screen in the back of each front headrest. This vehicle also has foldaway picnic tables that match the rest of its special wood trim.** NICK DIMBLEBY

LEFT: **Autobiography two-tone leather options were almost infinite in their scope, and could be eye-catching. The six-pleat leather pattern is nevertheless as used on mainstream Range Rovers of the time.** NICK DIMBLEBY

LATE AUTOBIOGRAPHY MODELS

By this time, the Autobiography programme was working well. It was producing special editions for multiple markets (although some overseas sales companies preferred to produce their own); it was providing a bespoke finishing service for customers at the top end of the market; and it was also beginning to focus on the possibilities for the third-generation Range Rover that would be due in late 2001.

The **Autobiography** programme was now in full swing, and could turn out radically different-looking interiors such as this one. **Of** course the basic hardware remained unchanged from standard. **In** this case, the **CARiN** screen is set to show the compass heading. NICK DIMBLEBY

BELOW: **Two-colour** upholstery became a popular **Autobiography** option, along with a steering wheel with a partial wood rim. This one also has a leather-trimmed dashboard to match the seats.

Even so, there were still new avenues to explore. According to an internal marketing document from 1999, the plan was to make available a Range Rover with an 8in (203mm) wheelbase stretch, and to offer armouring to B2/B4 levels as well. The idea of a stretched vehicle may well have been a casualty of the Ford purchase of Land Rover in summer 2000, and no prototype seems to have been built. However, a discreetly armoured Range Rover did become available from LRSV, and the vehicle seems to have been built in conjunction with S MacNeillie & Son Ltd of Walsall, who were the acknowledged British specialists in the business.

No details of this element of the Autobiography programme are available, for fairly obvious reasons, and it is quite likely that customers who ordered an armoured 38A from LRSV asked for the Autobiography badge to be omitted, in order to draw less attention to the vehicle. It is impossible to say whether LRSV's armoured 38A models used coil springs or had an uprated air-suspension system to deal with the extra weight of the armour plating. Nothing was said at the time, not least because it would obviously have been bad public relations to suggest that the standard air suspension was not up to the job!

What is clear is that at least one LRSV armoured Range Rover – for a customer in the Middle East – had twin side-hinged tail doors in place of the standard tailgate. MacNeillie had done the same with their armoured conversions of the first-generation Range Rover, not least because the weight of the armour made the standard horizontally split tailgate too heavy to manipulate. This vehicle was equipped with Discovery-pattern inward-facing folding seats in the load bay for the VIP's bodyguards, but of course these armoured Range Rovers were built to individual specification and others probably differed.

CHAPTER SEVEN

EMERGENCY SERVICE VEHICLES

The original Range Rover had been a big success with the emergency services, not least because Land Rover had offered specially extended chassis for ambulance use and a six-wheel chassis for airfield crash tender and fire service work. However, the philosophy behind that vehicle had been very different. In the early days, its makers had seen it as simply another model of Land Rover, to be exploited and developed just as the utility models always had been. The Range Rover 38A was never intended to follow that path: it was designed as a luxury car with off-road ability, and not as another workhorse model.

One result of that was that there would never be any dedicated 38A fire or crash-rescue vehicles. There were, of course, a few examples that were bought by fire services as commanders' vehicles, but not for front-line fire or rescue work. The cost of the basic vehicle, the complete absence of chassis-cab versions suitable for conversion, and the sheer complexity of such things as the electrical system, were all enough to deter even the bravest of the aftermarket specialists from attempting to produce such conversions.

AMBULANCE CONVERSIONS

Much the same set of considerations affected the ambulance market. The extended wheelbase Defender 130 was available for those who wanted a large ambulance with off-road ability, and the market for a more luxurious and inevitably much more expensive conversion based on the Range Rover was simply not there. None of that, however, prevented a French ambulance specialist from developing a prototype. In vindication of Land Rover's own assessment of the likely market, this prototype appears never to have attracted orders for production versions.

The company responsible was BSE (Bruno Scherer Entreprise SAS), which had been established in 1993 at Hendaye

The ambulance conversion by BSE in France added a GRP 'pod' to the standard vehicle, to give extra length plus a modicum of extra height within the body. NICK DIMBLEBY

The host vehicle for the French ambulance was an entry-level 2.5 DT. NICK DIMBLEBY

The additional length gave just enough room for a single gurney behind the driver's seat. NICK DIMBLEBY

The redundant rear door was used to give access to a stowage compartment for medical kit. NICK DIMBLEBY

in the Basque region. Today, BSE specializes in ambulance and hearse conversions, but in the mid-1990s it was a relatively new business and chose to explore the possibilities of a Range Rover ambulance conversion. The prototype was based on a left-hand-drive 2.5 DT model with a manual gearbox, although the company did advertise the availability of automatic transmission as an alternative.

The conversion was cleverly and neatly effected, with only minimal body modifications. BSE constructed a bulkhead behind the front seats, and extended the rear body behind the axle to create enough length for a stretcher to be carried. The centre of the roof was also raised by an add-on section which ran from front to rear and created additional headroom, and a number of items of medical equipment were added to the interior. Blackout glass in the rear doors, rearmost side windows and top tailgate completed the picture.

POLICE RANGE ROVERS

The original Range Rover had been enormously popular with police forces in the UK, and in some other countries as well. It had a lot to recommend it as a police motorway patrol car, which is the role that most examples bought by UK police forces fulfilled. It was capable of carrying the equipment that crews needed to deal with motorway incidents; it was rapid, with a high top speed; it gave crews good visibility all around; and it had enough low-down torque to pull (or sometimes push) stranded lorries off the main carriageway. On top of that, its off-road ability made it capable of driving across a motorway embankment to get around an obstruction if necessary. And it had the advantage of height to make it visible from a long distance, which was useful to give advance warning to traffic of an incident that required them to slow down.

Although the second-generation model was intended to establish the Range Rover more securely in the luxury market, Land Rover were well aware of the benefits of retaining those police sales. On the one hand, the public tended to assume that a vehicle used by the police must be reliable and well made, which provided a subtle but very valuable endorsement of the Range Rover's qualities. On the other hand, the presence of motorway patrol Range Rovers around the country was a constant reminder of the model's existence, which was another form of valuable publicity. The sheer numbers of police Range Rovers bought new also gave a welcome boost to overall sales of the model.

So right from the beginning, the design teams working on the new Range Rover had to bear in mind that a police specification variant would be among those required. The whole issue was so important that police representatives were invited to offer comments during the design and development stages of the 38A. The new model was first revealed to selected police forces in the summer of 1990 – before the first full prototypes had been built, and at a time when the project was known as Pegasus. One result of this was that many police forces referred to the new model as the 'Pegasus' throughout its production career, even though the project code-name had long since been changed at Land Rover.

By the time Pegasus was under development, the Range Rover was already facing competition from newer 4×4 estates with a similar design. In Scotland, the Northern Constabulary tried some Mercedes-Benz G-Wagens in 1988, and at about the same time the Leicestershire force bought the first of several Isuzu Troopers. During the early 1990s, the competition became fiercer still, as the Jeep Cherokee and Vauxhall Monterey (a British-built Isuzu design) came on to the market. Last but not least, Land Rover's own Discovery had started to claim a significant proportion of UK police sales after its introduction in 1989. The key attraction of most of these models was that they could do the Range Rover's job more cheaply, which was a major consideration. Sadly, it was also true that the reliability of the first-generation Range Rover had certainly not been exemplary, and these new pretenders promised better.

So Land Rover wasted no time in preparing police demonstrators of the new Range Rover. At least six were ready at launch time in autumn 1994, registered as M751 CVC to M753 CVC, M761, M762 CVC and M774 CVC.

Many police Range Rovers in the UK used the 'Battenburg' livery of reflective panels. Demonstrator M751 CVC was pictured while on loan to a northern British police force, and in the half-light the properties of those reflective panels are clear. The M-CVC demonstrator vehicles probably all had five-spoke (SE) wheels.
ROGER CONWAY

The first example of the new Range Rover to enter service with a British police force was Greater Manchester's N461 VVM. The wheels are the entry-level three-spoke alloys that were standardized for police vehicles.

All were 4.0-litre V8 petrol models, probably all had the manual gearbox, and they were completed with a generic police specification. The base vehicles were white, and all had the increasingly popular high-visibility 'Battenburg' decal livery. They had light bars on the roof, blue lights embedded in the radiator grille, and – because there was no obvious alternative – alloy wheels. Strangely, perhaps, these were the five-spoke design associated with the TL2 (SE and DSE) models rather than the three-spoke type used on entry-level variants.

These demonstrators quickly embarked on a series of loans to police forces all round the country. They soon attracted the orders that Solihull wanted, and were replaced after a year with a second fleet of vehicles that had the same

The Battenburg livery was far from universal, of course. This is one of the 1996 batch of demonstrators, N823 ARW, pictured while on loan to the Strathclyde Police. PVEC/ALAN MATTHEWS

The livery favoured by the Warwickshire Constabulary was different again. N492 XDU was a 1996 delivery. PVEC/ARC

ABOVE: **Greater Manchester's first 38A Range Rover was pictured with one of its 1997 deliveries when the latter was new.** NICK DIMBLEBY

The centre cubby box provided a convenient location for a police radio on this Greater Manchester vehicle.
NICK DIMBLEBY

One of Greater Manchester's 1997 deliveries was pictured here at the scene of an accident, preparing to tow the damaged car clear of the carriageway. NICK DIMBLEBY

purpose but, of course, carried newer N-prefix registration plates. The first six demonstrators were probably all sold to UK police forces, the most famous of them being M751 CVC, which was sold to London's Metropolitan Police. The Met allocated it to the Special Escort Group, and during 1997 it did duty in the funeral cortège of Diana, Princess of Wales.

An important element in the police specification that Land Rover developed was that it should deviate as little as possible from the standard production specification; this would obviously save manufacturing costs. So the Police Range Rover was really not much more than a low-specification vehicle with a few differences from standard that allowed each police force to make the modifications it wanted as easily as possible. There have always been rumours that the engine ECUs were specially modified to give better performance, but there seems to be no evidence that this was ever done at the Solihull factory. There certainly was a 'police specification' setting in the BECM, but all this really did was to take into account the electrical load placed on the system by additional police equipment.

By the time the first customer vehicles were delivered to UK police forces in early 1996, the specification seems to have been established around the 4.0-litre V8 engine, a manual gearbox, entry-level (cloth) upholstery, and three-spoke alloy wheels. It is interesting that the 4.6-litre engine did not feature in that list, and the likely reason is that the additional costs of the bigger-engined model were not justified by its additional performance. In an article in *Land Rover Enthusiast* magazine for December 2000, Peter Hall established that the very first 38A Range Rover to enter police ownership in the UK was N461 VMM, which reached the

P628 WNL was new to the Strathclyde Police, and is now part of the Heritage Collection at Gaydon. Although it looks much like any other motorway patrol Range Rover, in fact it was bought for special duties. NICK DIMBLEBY

P628 WNL looks perfectly standard from behind, but note the darker shadow around the top of the front door glass. NICK DIMBLEBY

Greater Manchester Police in February 1996. Other 1996 deliveries were made to Essex (who only ever had one), the City of London Police, the Lancashire Constabulary, the Cheshire Constabulary, the Warwickshire Constabulary and the Durham Constabulary.

In most cases, these initial orders were followed by orders for more, and during the later 1990s the 38A gradually took over completely from the first-generation Range Rover as Britain's most popular motorway patrol car. Generally speaking, it appears that the police crews had a lot of respect for them. Reliability was generally better than that of their predecessors; build quality was much higher; and the crews appreciated very much the ability to talk to one another at speeds above 75mph (120km/h) – which was next to impossible in the first-generation model because of wind noise.

The vehicle was marked up like ordinary police Range Rovers, but was actually far from ordinary. NICK DIMBLEBY

WARNING

Read this notice before driving the vehicle

This vehicle is fitted with 180-degree ballistic protection, which has increased the vehicle weight (rear protection is only to the driver and passenger seat backs). This has therefore affected the handling & braking capabilities.

The vehicle should only be driven at normal road speeds and not used for pursuit situations under any circumstances.

In the event of an emergency where the doors will not open, you should exit from the rear door windows or rear windscreen.

Your view may be slightly distorted through the front windscreen, due to the thickness of the ballistic glass.

TOP LEFT: **As the warning notice on the dashboard advises, the vehicle had '180-degree ballistic protection'. The front end was (fairly lightly) armoured, with an armoured windscreen and side door glasses. This altered the weight and balance, so that it did not handle like a standard motorway patrol Range Rover.** NICK DIMBLEBY

TOP RIGHT: **Police forces adapted switches to suit their needs. This one is in P628 WNL and would flash the headlights continuously – a signal typically used to persuade other drivers to move over and let the police vehicle through.** NICK DIMBLEBY

LEFT: **The typical motorway patrol Range Rover carried a variety of equipment for dealing with incidents. The racking was generally provided by each individual force to suit its own preferences. This is a West Midlands vehicle belonging to the Central Motorway Patrol Group.** A FORMER POLICEMAN

The typical police 38A lasted in service for between three and five years, and was then sold on to the civilian market with a mileage often not far short of 200,000 (320,000km). Over the years, some details of the basic police specification changed, and beginning with the R-registration (1998) model deliveries, the alloy wheels were the new and more stylish Futura entry-level types, while 2000 and later models typically had Typhoon alloys. As always, there were exceptions.

No definitive list exists of UK police forces that used the 38A Range Rover. However, the following list is as comprehensive as it is possible to be at the time of writing. It has been put together with input from Peter Hall and from PVEC (the Police Vehicle Enthusiasts' Club). Note that the Range Rovers of several Midlands forces worked together as members of the Central Motorway Patrol Group.

Avon & Somerset Police
Central Scotland Police

Cheshire Constabulary
City of London Police
Durham Constabulary
Gloucestershire Constabulary
Grampian Police
Greater Manchester Police
Gwent Police
Hampshire Constabulary
Kent Police
Lancashire Constabulary
Lothian & Borders Police
Metropolitan Police
Northern Constabulary
South Yorkshire Police
Sussex Police
Strathclyde Police
Warwickshire Police
West Midlands Police

Typhoon alloy wheels were standard wear on entry-level models for 1999, and therefore also on police Range Rovers. Gwent's T487 KDW, a 4.0-litre model, has them. PVEC/PB

This 1998 Range Rover belonging to the Strathclyde Police has another version of the Battenburg livery, and has the Futura alloy wheels that were then supplied as part of the police specification. PVEC/ALAN MATTHEWS

Typhoon alloy wheels figure again on T950 SSX, a 1999-specification model that belonged to Lothian & Borders. PVEC/ALAN MATTHEWS

Land Rover registered a large number of vehicles in the V-LOB series, and the Northern Constabulary's V136 LOB probably started life as a factory demonstrator. Although registered in late 1999 with a 2000-model registration, it has the older 1999-specification lights. PVEC/ALAN MATTHEWS

RIGHT: **Land Rover were clearly using up old-stock wheels for police models by the time of Y837 TVP, a 2001 model that was used by the Central Motorway Patrol Group. The wheels are 1999-specification Spyder alloys.** A FORMER POLICEMAN

BELOW: **Old-model Spyder alloys also feature on this 2001 model, Y838 TVP, a sister vehicle from the CMPG fleet. Both vehicles have large rubber 'pusher' bars on the front bumper, which were used to push stranded vehicles clear of the carriageway when there was no other practical option.** PVEC

CHAPTER EIGHT

BUILDING THE 38A RANGE ROVER

By the time the second-generation Range Rover came on stream, the Solihull factory consisted of three major blocks of buildings – the North Works, the South Works and the East Works. Within each of these major units, individual departments had their own areas, which were identified by numbers. So, for example, the old administrative offices were Block 1, located on the north side of the South Works, while Block 38A (where the Range Rover design team had been located) was on the south side of the same South Works.

As far as the Range Rover was concerned, the most important areas were in the North Works. This was divided into two main sections, one that was given over to engine assembly, and one that was the main assembly hall for the vehicle. The North Works was where the first-generation Range Rover had been built for most of its last sixteen years, although assembly of the last ones had been moved to a low-volume line elsewhere on the site to allow the lines for the second-generation model to be installed during 1994.

This aerial view over the Land Rover factory site at Solihull is taken from just beyond the Lode Lane entrance, looking roughly south-east. Range Rover assembly was in the North Works, the large group of buildings nearest the camera. The image dates from the 1990s; a lot has changed since then.

In the South Works, the areas relevant to the Range Rover were those where gearboxes and axles were assembled. The other main activity in the South Works was assembly of Defender and Discovery models.

The East Works was subdivided into three areas, all of them relevant to the Range Rover. At the eastern end was the Transmissions plant; next to that and in the middle of the building was the Body-In-White (BIW) plant (where bodies were put together from individual panels); and at the western end of the building was the Paint Shop, where the newly assembled bodies were painted before being transported to the final assembly lines in the North Works.

However, many of the components that made up a 38A Range Rover were not manufactured at Solihull, but were brought to the site by road from the factories where they were made. Of the major elements, the chassis frames were delivered as complete assemblies from John Thompson Pressings in Wolverhampton. The BMW diesel engines and ZF automatic gearboxes reached Solihull from their own assembly plants in Austria (Steyr) and Germany (Friedrichshaven) respectively. Body panels, of which there were 260 in every Range Rover, came from the Rover Body and Pressings plant at Swindon, formerly a Pressed Steel factory. Castings for the engines, manual gearboxes, transfer boxes, differentials and axles came from several outside suppliers, as did the smaller items such as electrical components, glass, tyres and so on.

MAJOR CHANGES

Land Rover invested very heavily in new buildings, new plant and new processes to ensure that the Range Rover 38A was built to the very highest standards the company could achieve. This was not simply a matter of corporate pride: it was an essential requirement for a car that was going to compete for sales with top-class luxury saloons from BMW, Lexus and Mercedes-Benz.

A total of £15 million was invested to prepare the 6,600sq m (71,000sq ft) BIW plant within the East Works for assembling the 38A bodyshell, which was constructed very differently indeed from that used on the first-generation Range Rover. A further £3 million went into the Paint Shop, which as a result had become one of the largest of its kind in the UK.

The improvements to Solihull's existing Paint Shop had included new overhead conveyors, a new colour application machine, a new underseal booth, a new surface distribution system and a new anti-chip application area. Other facilities had been uprated or relocated to make better use of the existing building, such as the electrostatic application and the sealer line. The inspection line had also been extended and its lighting improved to allow for better quality control.

A great deal of effort had also gone into the control of fumes, contamination and dust within the Paint Shop, in order to achieve the best possible working environment for a top quality paint finish. To this end, all ancillary equipment and plant not directly involved in the various processes was kept carefully isolated.

In the engine-build area of the North Works, new crankshaft and conrod machining lines had been put in as part of the plant upgrades. The transmission assembly area in the South Works had also undergone a major re-fit in late 1993 and early 1994 to cater for the introduction of the new R380 gearbox, which would be shared by all Solihull's models.

However, the biggest investment – over £13 million – had gone into the Trim and Final Assembly area within the North Works. This vast assembly hall covered an area of 35,000sq m (376,600sq ft), and when 38A production began in 1994, the North Works assembly line represented state-of-the-art technology for hand-building motor vehicles.

Even though assembly techniques had become far more sophisticated since the early days of the original Range Rover, there was still plenty of human involvement in the assembly process. Other manufacturers were increasingly relying on robots to deliver consistent quality on their assembly lines, but there was in fact only one robot in the North Works, and that was in the glazing cell. Nevertheless, the human involvement in building a 38A Range Rover was very different from the human involvement traditionally associated with car manufacture.

Right from the start, the new assembly lines had been designed to eliminate the need for excessive stretching and bending, the activities that most commonly resulted in strain and other injuries to assembly line workers. Land Rover had also drawn on the experience that the Rover Group had gained when ergonomics consultants advised on the design of the Rover 600 assembly plant at Cowley.

So among the key features of the new lines was the large quantity of 'helpers' and power-assisted machinery, which made it easier to lift and locate heavy items such as doors, wheels, sunroofs, seating and dashboards. These assisters had been specially developed to take the weight of components while a lineside worker – 'associate', in Land Rover terminology, see sidebar – guided them into place.

PEOPLE POWER

Land Rover used the new Range Rover assembly lines to introduce new approaches to working at its Solihull factory. There were new management theories in the air, too, and many of these had been borrowed from Honda – the Japanese company with which the cars side of the Rover Group was working closely before the BMW take-over in 1994. In the assembly halls of the new Range Rover, there were no 'assembly line staff': instead, the members of the workforce were dignified with the title of 'associates'.

Despite all this new technology, there was no substitute for the human element. Assembly of the new Range Rover had begun with a pilot-build phase, during which the line ran more slowly than it would during full production so that snags could be identified and eliminated. The team that assembled the pilot-production vehicles, beginning in late 1993, was able to advise on the ideal height at which vehicles should progress down the assembly line, and their views were taken into account before volume production began. Advice from the same team resulted in the bins and racks

containing parts for fitting being placed where they could most easily be reached alongside the assembly line. All this in turn reduced the physical stresses of the assembly process to a large degree, and allowed the assembly line staff to concentrate on building a quality vehicle.

BUILDING THE BODIES

The start of the build process for the 38A Range Rover was in the Body In White (BIW) plant that was located within the East Works. This plant could turn out a minimum of sixteen bodyshells per hour.

The body panels arrived at the Solihull BIW plant from the body and pressings plant at Swindon, many of them with weld nuts already fitted in preparation for the later stages of assembly. All were delivered as individual panels except for the bonnet, which came as a complete assembly with the outer skin already attached to the frame.

Range Rover bodies began to take shape in fourteen sub-assembly zones within the framing area. Here, the incoming panels were jigged and welded manually to create the six main constituents of the body frame – the front end, the main floor, the rear floor, the two body sides and the roof. There were, of course, two alternative roof panels, one with

The Range Rover shell used large monoside pressings, and one is seen here in the BIW plant. NICK DIMBLEBY

A bodyshell comes together on the line in the BIW plant. Welding was by automated trackside robots. NICK DIMBLEBY

Completed 38A shells emerge from the BIW plant on their way to the Paint Shop. NICK DIMBLEBY

Bodyshells for all Land Rover products were 'marshalled' in a single area before entering the paint plant. Examples of the Defender and Discovery can be seen alongside the 38A here. NICK DIMBLEBY

an aperture for a sunroof and one without. A total of 120 jigs and more than 140 welding guns were used at this stage of manufacture.

The sub-assemblies were then fed on to the main framing line, which was fully automated. Here, they passed through nine stations to emerge as recognizable Range Rover bodies – though at this stage still without doors and tailgate. Each bodyshell consisted of an inner steel frame to which were fitted aluminium alloy outer panels – although the finished result was more of a monocoque than the body of the original Range Rover, which had used a different 'skeleton frame' construction. Bodies were automatically jigged using pins and clamps, and each one received sixty welds. The cycle time for this part of the assembly process was 3.3min per body.

Each body then moved on to the robot weld station, where two robots applied another 264 welds. These two robots automatically changed their welding heads three times during the process cycle, thus in effect doing the job

of six robots. The bodies then passed to a manual finish weld stage, where those welds not accessible to the robots were completed by assembly line staff.

Meanwhile, the doors and tailgate frames were assembled separately. Their build process involved thirty-one jigs and twenty-three welding guns, followed by six power clinches, which fixed their aluminium skins to the frame assemblies. Doors, tailgates, bonnets and wings all then met up with the completed body-frame assemblies on a final line, where they were fitted and set to the correct clearances. Although the doors would be removed again at a later stage in the assembly process, the system ensured that they would be refitted to the shell from which they had been taken to avoid later fitting problems.

Finally, a team of inspectors carried out a cosmetic inspection under high-intensity lighting, and the completed bodies passed on to a lift which took them out of the BIW plant into the adjacent paint shop.

Doors were removed so that the paint could get into all those areas of the body they would otherwise mask; the doors were sprayed alongside the shell they came from. These are shells fresh from the paint plant. NICK DIMBLEBY

PAINTING THE BODIES

The Paint Shop was situated on three floors of a self-contained building that was linked to the assembly areas by conveyors. Range Rover bodies arriving from the BIW plant entered the Paint Shop on the ground floor. By this time, every body had been allocated to an order – which might have been a specific customer order that had come in from a dealer, or in some cases was an order 'for stock'. So the Paint Shop's first task was to 'sequence' the bodies – to order them into batches so that those destined to be a particular colour would go through the spray booths together. This reduced the number of times the process had to be stopped while spray heads were changed and equipment cleaned to take a different paint colour.

However, the colour-painting process was still some time away at this stage. After 'sequencing', bodies were held in buffer zones on the ground floor until it was time for their batch to be taken by conveyor up to the first floor, where the body-coating process began.

The first stage in this process was corrosion protection. The bodyshells were coated with zinc phosphate in an eight-stage spray process. This zinc coating had two main purposes: first it was to act as a protective barrier against penetrating stone damage – if the zinc coating itself became damaged, it would oxidize to form a protective layer in a process known as 'sacrificial protection'. The coating's sec-ond main purpose was to prevent the electrolytic corrosion that can take place when two different metals are bonded together – such as the steel and aluminium alloy used in the Range Rover bodyshell.

Further corrosion protection was then provided by PVC seam sealing and underbody coating. Each body also received additional stone-chip treatment to vulnerable areas, such as the leading edge of the bonnet, the roof, and the front and rear wheel arches. Only then did the actual paint process begin, when a high-build primer-surfacer paint was applied by remotely controlled high-voltage electrostatic equipment.

The primed bodies then passed through a drying area, and on to the final paint area. Here they received two coats of the final colour, again from high-voltage electrostatic spray equipment; these were followed by a coat of tough, clear lacquer designed to give both a deep shine and high durability. All these coats were applied using an environmentally friendly water-based process.

The last stage in each body's progress through the Paint Shop was then a trip to the top floor by conveyor, where the new paint was dried in stoving ovens.

ENGINE AND TRANSMISSION ASSEMBLY

While the bodies were being assembled and painted, engines

Meanwhile, the chassis was assembled on a separate line. Here, the axles are in position on the special 'cradle' that will take the vehicle through to nearly the end of the assembly line. NICK DIMBLEBY

The chassis has been lowered on to the axles, and suspension and other components are already in place as the chassis line proceeds. NICK DIMBLEBY

The engine and transmission being lowered in, still on the chassis line. Note the mounting of the transfer box on the left of the main gearbox – unique in Land Rover products at that time. NICK DIMBLEBY

and transmissions were being assembled in other parts of the Solihull factory complex. As explained above, the raw castings for the Range Rover's V8 engines arrived in the North Works engine build plant from outside suppliers, where they were first machined and heat treated as necessary.

From the machine shops, components then passed to the assembly area, where both 4.0-litre and 4.6-litre engines went down the same line. This was not the only line in the building: there were also lines for the 300Tdi diesel engines, and, in a dedicated separate area, for the L-series diesel initially used in Rover cars but from 1997 also in the Land Rover Freelander.

Each engine was built on an automatic guided trolley that moved from station to station following magnetic coils embedded in the floor of the building. These trolleys had sensors that automatically brought them to a halt if they hit an obstruction – such as an errant human being. Assembly still depended on line-side workers, but the assembly plant was far more automated than in earlier times, with multi-spindle nut runner and torque units to aid assembly of cylinder heads, conrod joints, main bearing caps and sump pans.

At the end of the build process, engines were sent for testing before being mated with their gearbox. This testing involved a twenty-minute 'cold cycle' test, when the engine was connected to an electric motor. This allowed it to 'run' without the need to introduce volatile petrol into the working environment. Once signed off as satisfactory, complete engines were then moved into another area of the North Works to await their gearboxes and transfer boxes.

Most 38A Range Rovers had automatic gearboxes, which of course were shipped into the assembly area from outside. However, the manual gearboxes were simply transported across the factory from their assembly area on the south side of the South Works, behind the Discovery and Defender assembly lines. Completed gearboxes were tested before leaving the South Works, and were mated to their transfer boxes in an assembly area within the North Works.

The North Works was also fed with axle and differential assemblies from the South Works. The raw castings of course came into Solihull from outside, and were machined and heat-treated as necessary on site before joining the assembly line. Each axle then took about an hour to travel along the assembly line before being checked and sent to the chassis assembly area in the North Works.

TRIM AND FINAL ASSEMBLY

Everything finally came together in the North Works, home of the trim and final assembly area. This consisted of a chassis build line and a body line, which eventually converged as the final line, and several line-side sub-assembly build and test areas.

The chassis build line was where the engine, transmission, axles, brakes, steering, suspension and fuel tank were assembled to the chassis frame. While this process was being carried out, painted bodies were being prepared for the final line after their arrival from the Paint Shop.

Two important processes were carried out as bodies entered the North Works. First, they were loaded on to the moving conveyors in strict order so they would meet the correct trim and engine on the assembly line. In addition, each body was fitted with protective panels to safe-

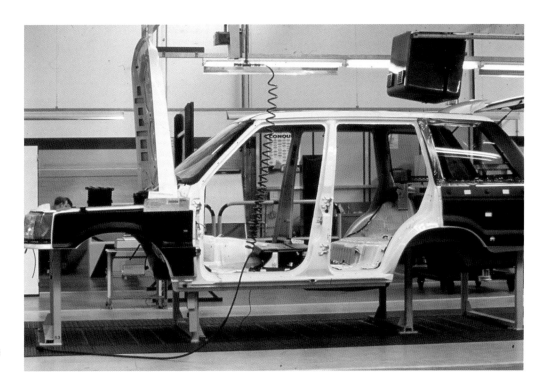

The scene now shifts to the trim and final assembly line, where protective cladding is put on the bodyshell to prevent damage to the paint. The headlights and front indicators are already in place here.

Dashboards arrived in fully assembled form from an outside supplier. This one is being prepared for fitting. NICK DIMBLEBY

BELOW: **The doors progressed along their own line, keeping pace with the body they came from. This pair will soon be fitted with its interior trim cards.**

ABOVE: **Dashboards in, the bodyshells pass further along the line. Note how batches of a single colour are grouped together: it made for an easier life in the Paint Shop.** NICK DIMBLEBY

RIGHT: **Final preparation of seats was also done alongside the main trim and final line.** NICK DIMBLEBY

guard against accidental damage to the paint finish during the assembly process.

As each body entered the body line, its doors were removed and placed on to their own 'cradle'. This cradle then travelled round its own assembly line within the North Works, and glass, winder motors, speakers and trim were fitted before the doors rejoined their original body towards the end of the assembly sequence.

Meanwhile, the doorless bodies were going through stations for underbody assembly work, electrical wiring, sunroof panels (where needed) and glazing. The facia panels, supplied by a sub-contractor as fully assembled units, were also installed. Once all these items were in place, the

Everybody's favourite assembly moment: the 'marriage', or body drop, where body and chassis finally meet. The bodies were brought into position by overhead conveyor, still without doors.

Special handling equipment was needed to help in installing the heavy seats.

With the seats now in, the whole assembly began to look like a **Range Rover.** NICK DIMBLEBY

The doors, now with their interior trim cards, went back on once the seats were in place and there was no more major work to be done on the interior.

Handling equipment was used again to make the task of fitting the wheels more manageable.

This is close to the end of the line. The wheels have not yet touched the ground, but the assembly operation is over. NICK DIMBLEBY

Each completed vehicle went through a series of tests before being 'bought off'. This one was going through an air-conditioning test.

partially completed bodies were then carried by overhead conveyor to the mount line at the end of the chassis build line, where bodies were lowered on to chassis assemblies and the two were bolted together.

The body and chassis assemblies now passed down the final line. Here, each one had seating fitted, engine coolant and brake fluids were added, and the bumpers, doors and wheels were fitted. An interesting aspect of this was that the seats were completed on a sub-assembly line alongside the final line. Right at the end of the process, fuel was put into the Range Rover's tank and the vehicle was driven off the end of the line.

The final stage was a series of tests and calibrations. The brakes were tested on a rolling road, there were tests for water sealing and for the electrical systems, the air suspension would be calibrated and the steering would be set up. Once each vehicle had been 'bought off' – had passed its inspection – it was then driven to a despatch area within the factory grounds for onward shipment to a Land Rover dealer.

The bright lights indicate the final inspection bay, and would highlight any flaws in the paintwork.

CHAPTER NINE

AFTERMARKET SPECIALS

Several aftermarket companies had made a comfortable living by providing enhancements to the first-generation Range Rover. A demand for improvements to the basic vehicle had arisen within a few years of its introduction in 1970, and by the middle of the 1970s there was a thriving industry that produced seemingly ever more extravagant luxury conversions, particularly for the Middle East.

It took Land Rover several years to catch up and to begin to offer the sort of luxury appointments that customers clearly wanted in their Range Rovers, and although the factory never equalled the extremes of the aftermarket converters, it did create tastefully luxurious vehicles that had a wide appeal. However, the lessons of the 1970s were well learned, and by the end of the 1980s Land Rover was determined to claw back as much of the aftermarket business as possible. It did so very successfully, and one result was that there were far fewer aftermarket conversions of the 38A Range Rover than there had been of its predecessor.

Nevertheless, there was still room for some aftermarket specialists to work on the second-generation Range Rover. There were armoured conversions, high-performance conversions, and even a few no-expense-spared conversions for the Middle East in the time-honoured fashion.

ARMOURED VEHICLES

By the time of the second-generation Range Rover, there was a small but steady demand from around the world for armoured limousines. The purpose of such vehicles was mainly to protect the VIP or VIPs that they carried against armed attack, either as a prelude to a kidnap or an assassination. They were usually described as 'discreetly armoured', which meant that they looked like standard vehicles so they would not attract attention. In practice, of course, a close look would reveal considerable differences, but from a distance or to the casual observer there was nothing unusual

about them. The armour plating was concealed behind standard outer panels, and the armoured glass was not immediately obvious.

These vehicles were necessarily expensive. As a guide, the lowest level of armour plating was likely to add around £80,000 to the cost of a Range Rover in the later 1990s, while the very top level would probably add £170,000 – and these figures, of course, were on top of the initial purchase price of the vehicle. That level of cost, plus the specialist nature of the conversions, ensured that an armoured Range Rover was never a very common sight.

Although Land Rover Special Vehicles eventually put such a vehicle on to the market through its Autobiography programme (see Chapter 6), other vehicle armouring specialists had already developed armoured Range Rovers to meet the demand. The earliest of these was probably the one produced by the Jankel Group, at Weybridge in Surrey. This company had worked on first-generation Range Rovers, building a number of special four-door conversions for Libya in the days before four-door models could be bought from the showroom floor. The Jankel Group received its first enquiries about modifying the 38A Range Rover as early as 1995, and would go on to build a number of extensively customized examples (see below) as well as armoured types.

Founder Robert Jankel had been involved in custom building since 1955, and had been behind the Panther car company in the mid-1970s (which was later sold to a Korean owner). By the mid-1990s, however, Jankel had strong contacts with major companies that included Rolls-Royce, and was dedicated to high-end conversions and adaptations, many of which were formidably expensive. Jankel's first armoured Range Rover took more than a year of research and development to create, beginning in the early part of 1996. The conversion was brought to market in 1997, and substituted coil springs for the standard air suspension, which Jankel considered was not capable of dealing with the additional weight of the armour plate.

Fixed side glasses were often a giveaway feature of the armoured vehicles. This one was built by Mondiale Security in France for a UK customer.

Several other specialist companies became involved with armoured Range Rovers – and as Chapter 6 explains, Land Rover did so themselves eventually. As examples of those other companies, the German tuner Arden (based in Krefeld) linked up with MBB Security Cars in 1998 to build an armoured Range Rover, which it displayed at that year's Security '98 exhibition in Essen. Whether Arden and MBB ever built any others is not clear. Mondiale Security Ltd in France also armoured at least one vehicle, which was examined by the author for a feature in the May 2008 issue of *Land Rover Enthusiast* magazine.

Most armoured Range Rovers must have been based on 4.6-litre models, because those had the extra power and torque to deal with the additional weight of the armour plating. Realistically, it is likely that few of them will survive in the longer term. As weapons and attack techniques have changed, so the type of armour needed has had to change, with the result that vehicles with an older specification become useless for their original role. Their poor fuel consumption and the impracticality of their heavy doors and other features have also deterred individuals from buying armoured Range Rovers as ordinary cars, with the result that many have simply been left to rot when they have fallen out of use.

HIGH PERFORMANCE RANGE ROVERS

As 'chip tuning', or modifying the engine-control software, became common during the 1990s, it was inevitable that the chip developers should turn their attention to the Range Rover. Demand was mostly for improved performance from the BMW diesel engine, which struggled a little with the weight of the 38A model, and so performance chips became (and remain) quite common for these vehicles. However, the inevitable demand for the ultimate in high performance also arose not long after the second-generation Range Rover reached the market, and specialist companies were only too willing to oblige. The costs, however, were high.

JE Engineering

Coventry-based JE Engineering appears to have been first on to the market with a high-performance Range Rover, with its Range Rover 'S' conversion in autumn 1996. This company had a long involvement with the Rover V8 engine, having originally been associated with V8 engine

Supercharging the
4.6-litre engine was
the performance
solution adopted by JE
Engineering: this was
the first example of the
S500 conversion.

The Eaton supercharger
nestled neatly under the
bonnet of the S500.

specialist John Eales, and had recently taken on Spen King, father of the original Range Rover and now retired, as a consultant.

The 'S' conversion depended on a heavily reworked 4.6-litre V8 engine equipped with a supercharger and inter-cooler. Maximum power went up to around 360bhp, and braking and suspension upgrades were available to complement this massive power increase.

However, the 'S' conversion was expensive and attracted few buyers. So JE Engineering developed a less expensive and less powerful derivative which they announced in February 1998 as the S500 model. Once again supercharged, its 4.6-litre engine boasted 315bhp and 500Nm (368lb/ft) of torque – that figure explaining the 500 in the model designation. The company claimed 0–60mph acceleration in 7.4sec, and a maximum speed of over 130mph (209km/h).

The S500 conversion was announced to coincide with JE Engineering's twenty-fifth anniversary, and the engine was priced at £15,995 plus VAT, inclusive of fitting. Inevitably, the S500 itself remained rare, but it did serve to draw attention to JE Engineering's ability to produce a high-performance Range Rover. The company went on to offer engine-management chip upgrades and a full range of accessories, and equipped several vehicles to a lower level of performance for satisfied customers.

Overfinch

Overfinch had become the leading aftermarket specialists in high-performance Range Rovers during the production of the first-generation model. Their 'trademark' was the use of a General Motors 5.7-litre (350cu in) small-block V8, as used in US cars such as the Chevrolet Corvette. It was only to be expected that they would transfer this technology to the second-generation model, and develop cosmetic and equipment upgrades to suit their customers as well.

Development work began almost as soon as the company's engineers were able to get their hands on a 38A, but it took around three years to get the vehicle right, and, most importantly, for the market to be ready for it. Overfinch announced what they called their 570 HSE model in May 1998, in the meantime continuing to fit their 5.7-litre engines into late-model first-generation Range Rovers, which satisfied customers who wanted a Range Rover with better performance than the latest 4.6 HSE.

The engine that went into the 570 HSE was the third-generation Overfinch derivative of the General Motors V8. Later developed further, in 1998 guise it delivered 330bhp at 4,700rpm with 425lb/ft of torque at 3,150rpm. This gave an Overfinch 570 HSE a maximum speed in excess of 130mph (209km/h) and, according to the company's own figures, a 0–60mph time of 7.2sec. That was considerably better than a standard 4.6 HSE, which peaked at 125mph (201km/h) and needed 9.3sec to reach 60mph from rest.

That these figures were not as impressive as those available from a first-generation Overfinch Range Rover with the same engine was the result of a combination of factors. Not least of these was the additional weight of the 38A. In fact, the 38A never did become as popular with Overfinch customers as the earlier model, and there was no doubt that it never offered quite the same driving qualities.

One major problem lay in the ride and handling. While Overfinch were able to stiffen up the air-suspension settings so that the vehicle did not wallow as much as a standard 38A, the 570 HSE never felt quite as taut as an Overfinch-converted first-generation Range Rover on steel springs. The steering was never as good, either; much to Overfinch's regret, the makers of the 38A's steering box were simply not interested in making a quicker ratio version of the standard steering box in small volumes, and it proved impossible to find a cost-effective alternative. So the standard, rather vague steering remained unchanged.

Nevertheless, handling did improve, partly thanks to the modified air suspension and partly because Overfinch recommended bigger tyres. These were Avon Turbospeed 255/60 WR 16s, as developed for the Bentley Turbo, which gave excellent adhesion and a first-rate ride, even on the standard 16in wheels. However, they were not suitable for off-road use, and 570 HSE customers who wanted to use their vehicles off-road were advised to have a second set of wheels available with all-terrain tyres fitted.

In creating a bespoke vehicle, Overfinch went beyond simply uprating the performance: their customers could also choose from a wide range of exterior and interior cosmetic upgrades. Thus, the earliest 570 HSE demonstrator had a front apron and mirror bodies painted to match the exterior (before all these were introduced as standard features in the UK), plus colour-coded five-spoke HSE alloy wheels. The replacement of the Land Rover ovals front and rear by Overfinch's own discreet black oval badge was standard, but the 'Overfinch 570 HSE' decal badge that replaced the original 4.6 HSE badge on the tailgate could be left off if a customer preferred other drivers not to know that the vehicle had a high-performance conversion.

Interior changes included contrasting piping on the seats and door trims, extra burr-walnut trim on the centre console, a wood-and-leather steering-wheel rim, chromed door release handles, and padded elbow-rests on all four doors. Many of these features could, of course, be obtained later from Land Rover, although Overfinch had them first. A further option was a set of instruments with black markings on white dial faces, intended to reflect the style seen in some high-performance sports cars.

However, development was always a continuous process for Overfinch, and by the end of 2000, an even more powerful and better handling 38A derivative was ready for launch. Formally announced at the Essen Motor Show in December 2000 (although at least six had already been ordered before then), it was called the Overfinch 630R Anniversary. This name reflected both the engine size and the fact that Overfinch was celebrating twenty-five years of specialization in high-performance Range Rovers – those twenty-five years

of course including the company's pre-1985 existence for ten years as Schuler.

The key feature of the 630R Anniversary was its new engine, which was a long-stroke development of the 5.7-litre GM engine with a swept volume of 6276cc (or 6.3 litres in round figures). This hand-built engine delivered 400bhp at 5,000rpm and 457lb/ft of torque at 3,200rpm, and gave the 630R a 0–60 mph standing start time of 6.61sec and a maximum speed of 138mph (222km/h).

To cope with the huge increase in engine torque, the control unit of the ZF four-speed automatic in the host 4.6 HSE Range Rover was re-programmed, although the transmission itself was strong enough to need no reinforcement. The braking system had also been uprated, with massive 366mm ventilated and cross-drilled front discs and four-piston alloy calipers. Specially developed for the job, these brakes carried the Overfinch logo on their calipers, and every vehicle that had them was supplied with a spare set of the special brake pads in case replacement became necessary miles from a supplier. These brakes gave superb stopping power,

Past masters Overfinch built a limited quantity of their 630R model to coincide with their twenty-fifth year in business. The engine was a 6.3-litre derivative of the GM 5.7-litre V8 that was the staple of their business.

This special decal was drawn up for the 630R models – but of course it would be left off if that was what a customer preferred.

The Overfinch engines carried a special build plate. This was number 2 of their 6.3-litre V8s.

and tests at the Millbrook Proving Ground proved they could haul the 630R down from 100mph (160km/h) to a dead stop in just 4.7sec.

On the road, the 630R was an astoundingly quick car, and in fact that 0–60mph acceleration made it quicker than a Porsche Boxster Tiptronic (0–60 in 7.3sec) or a Bentley Turbo RT (6.7sec). Only fractionally quicker was a Jaguar XK8, which needed 6.6sec to reach 60mph from a standstill. However, it suffered from the perennial problem of the standard steering with its woolly feel, with the result that the 630R always felt like the big car it really was. While it could be thrown about with confidence once a driver had become used to it, it was not a vehicle that inspired that confidence from the start.

Interior enhancements had also moved on, and by the time of the 630R Overfinch was offering hand-stitched leather upholstery in a style designed to resemble a Bentley Turbo, with centre and outer panels in contrasting colours. The dashboard could be brightened up with aluminium highlights, and there was highly polished grey birdseye maple for the wood trim. An Alpine satellite navigation system and grey suede headlining made up the 630R's interior specification. Outside, meanwhile, a neat new front apron moulding was painted to match the body colour, as were the grille bars, and the driving lamps were masked off to give them a distinctive oval shape.

Just twenty-five examples of the 630R Anniversary were built, to match those twenty-five years of business, but the individual components that made up the vehicle remained available as part of the Overfinch bespoke manufacturing service. The Anniversary models were distinguished by a discreet laurel-wreath logo just above the turn signal repeater lamps on the front wings.

Overfinch were, of course, well aware of the handling defects of the 38A, and spent a good deal of time and effort developing an electronically controlled active-ride system for the model. By all accounts, this allowed the vehicle to be driven like a much smaller sports car, and from that point of view was a huge success. However, it did not become a commercial success. When announced in mid-2001, it cost in the region of £10,000, which was more than even the typical wealthy Overfinch customer was prepared to pay – especially just before the third-generation Range Rover was due to reach the showrooms. Overfinch's efforts to get the price down to more acceptable levels proved in vain, and as a result no more than a handful of Overfinch 38As were ever fitted with the active-ride system.

After 38A production ended in 2001, Overfinch continued to offer its bespoke performance and cosmetic enhancements for the 38A Range Rover for a time. However, the company gradually moved on to offer high-performance derivatives of the third-generation (L322) Range Rover instead, as demand for 38A conversions dried up.

Other Performance Conversions

Much less well known than either JE Engineering or Overfinch were ADI Engineering of Bedford, who entered the high-performance 38A market in 1998. However, the company only converted small numbers of Range Rovers, and went into receivership in early 2000.

ADI offered upgraded derivatives of all three engines available in the standard model. A re-chip of the 2.5-litre diesel's engine-management system took power up to 177bhp and promised an extra 50 per cent of torque. For the 4.0-litre V8, the company claimed that its supercharger conversion raised power to around 243bhp, while torque increased to 292lb/ft. For the 4.6-litre engine, the chosen method of increasing performance was with a turbocharger, and in tandem with an intercooler, this gave 380bhp at 4,900rpm and 466lb/ft at 3,670rpm.

German tuners, including Arden, offered various performance enhancements for the 38A Range Rover, as well as some bespoke cosmetic items. Meanwhile, other performance enhancements were unique to the US market, as explained later.

CUSTOM BUILDING

Even though there were nowhere near as many radical conversions of the 38A as there had been of the first-generation Range Rover, such conversions were certainly carried out. Mainly, they were done for extremely wealthy customers in the Middle East. Although there were probably small numbers of conversions from other companies, the two leading British custom conversion specialists during the production life of the 38A Range Rover were the Jankel Group and Vantagefield.

Jankel

Most of Jankel's clients for custom-built Range Rovers were in the Middle East, and, as was typical in this market, some of the conversions were one-offs that were astronomically expensive. In mid-1998, a simple stretch that added more interior room within the body was likely to cost at

Jankel had a six-wheel conversion that was built for overseas customers. This is a late 1990s estate conversion.
NICK DIMBLEBY

A Jankel six-wheel model is seen here in build at the company's Weybridge premises. NICK DIMBLEBY

This Jankel six-wheeler was built with elevating seats as a hunting vehicle for desert use. NICK DIMBLEBY

least £40,000, while the company's six-wheel conversions started at £70,000. These prices were additional to the first cost of the Range Rover being converted – £51,165 at the time for a 4.6-litre HSE, which was usually the host model. If the interior was expensively customized – as it was very likely to be – the cost would, of course, increase commensurately.

Jankel's six-wheel conversion formed the basis of many different custom-built Range Rovers. Some were primarily intended to carry more passengers, and to this end they had raised rooflines so that the passengers sitting above the twin rear axles had sufficient headroom. Others were opened up and equipped as hunting vehicles – hunting, in

this case, being primarily the sport of falconry as practised in the desert. In this, the owner of the falcon will be driven in pursuit of the bird across the sands as it tracks its prey, and one or more seats in the pursuit vehicle are arranged to elevate so that the bird can more easily be kept in sight through binoculars.

The Jankel six-wheel Range Rovers were probably all built with the company's selectable six-wheel-drive system. This involved the addition of an extra transfer box driven from the differential of the second (original rear) axle. From here, drive was taken to the third axle by means of a specially made propshaft. Drive to that third axle could be selected electrically by means of a simple press-switch on the dashboard. On

This view looking forwards inside the Jankel hunting vehicle gives an idea of how the seats were arranged. There was a built-in coolbox, too. NICK DIMBLEBY

There was no front passenger seat. Instead, there was lounging room for the passenger in the seat behind. Note the armrest on the outboard side. NICK DIMBLEBY

A discreet badge on the Jankel vehicles indicated that all six wheels could be driven. NICK DIMBLEBY

LEFT: **The driver had the front compartment to themselves, the right-hand side being lounging room for the passenger behind.** NICK DIMBLEBY

ordinary roads, the vehicle would be driven in 6×4 mode, with just the front and centre axles driven, but drive to the third axle would be selected when the going got tougher.

Other 38A Range Rovers converted by Jankel included armoured vehicles on the standard wheelbase (see above) and a 42in (107cm) stretch with three rows of seats and six doors. The company also drew up plans for a 36in (91cm) stretch, which retained just four doors and provided lounging room for the occupants of the rear seats, but it is not clear whether the vehicle was ever built.

Vantagefield

Among the established companies that had made their name by custom-building first-generation Range Rovers was London-based Vantagefield. However, the boom in Range Rover conversions was over by the time of the 38A, and such vehicles formed only a small element of Vantagefield's business in the 1990s. As the company's David Linder explained in an interview with the author in 2015:

> The Land Rover market [in the Middle East] crashed and died when they introduced the 38A Range Rover. We did five of them with minor mods for the Crown Prince of Abu Dhabi, but he never bought another from us. People stopped using Range Rovers for hunting, and we moved on to Nissans and Toyotas because that's what they wanted.
>
> We still did a few luxury Range Rover mods for the Middle East, though. In fact, I think our ultimate Range Rover conversion was actually on a 38A. It was a white six-wheel stretch convertible and was a present from one Saudi prince to his brother.

A fairly basic Vantagefield conversion, which added a 5.0-litre John Eales V8 engine and steel springs to a low-specification model with cloth seats. Note also the rollover bar running through the dashboard. VANTAGEFIELD

Some of the first Vantagefield 38As had only limited body modifications, such as one that allowed the rear-door drop-glasses to sink fully into the doors. Others had uprated engines and coil springs instead of air suspension, which it appears that many clients in the Middle East initially distrusted.

Typical of the less extensive Vantagefield 38A conversions was a hunting vehicle based on a left-hand-drive 4.6 HSE. This had a John Eales-built 5.0-litre V8 engine, coil springs, and a large opening roof, which allowed occupants to stand in the vehicle and watch the progress of falcons and other birds of prey used for sport in the desert.

That 'ultimate' conversion that David Linder remembered was built in 2001, and was delivered in the late spring of that year. The conversion took around six months to complete, and began with the body's removal from the chassis. The chassis itself was then extended so that it would be possible to provide lounging room for the rear-seat passengers. To

Vantagefield built just one of these extended-wheelbase Range Rovers, for a UK client. VANTAGEFIELD

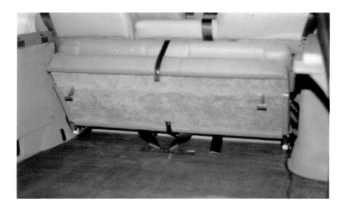

This was a far less expensive way of getting extra seating capacity from Vantagefield, although the folding rear seat faced backwards and was for occasional use only.

The Vantagefield long-wheelbase vehicle provided an additional two seats in a middle row; the rear bench seat remained in place further back. VANTAGEFIELD

The convertible top was power-operated, of course; this view indicates that it was a superb fit as well. VANTAGEFIELD

cope with the extra length, a third axle was fitted, and as this vehicle was to be used in the desert, selectable drive was provided to that axle. The air suspension was replaced by conventional steel coil springs, and a 5.0-litre V8 was fitted in place of the 4.6-litre original.

Next, the roof was removed from the body, and a brace was fitted between the B pillars at roof height to restore rigidity. The rear of the body was carefully strengthened, and a separate 'boot' was created behind the passenger compartment. A power-operated full-length convertible top was added to complete the basic conversion.

This six-wheel convertible was one of the last 38A conversions from Vantagefield; it was built in 2001. VANTAGEFIELD

The Vantagefield six-wheel convertible was designed to provide luxury above all else; it had only four seats, the main focus being on the rear pair. VANTAGEFIELD

Further work focused on the interior, which featured additional wood trim and special centre consoles front and rear, plus a whole range of entertainment units, satellite navigation and communications equipment. As a final touch, a winch was fitted to the front, just in case the vehicle ever got into difficulty in the desert sands. This spectacular vehicle was probably one of the very last of the major 38A custom conversions.

THE BRUNEI 'SPECIALS'

One particularly interesting footnote in the Range Rover 38A story relates to six examples that were allegedly used as the basis of some very special bespoke vehicles created for the Sultan of Brunei or for his brother, Prince Jefri. However, none of the parties supposedly involved in their creation has ever made an official comment on the story, so the version that appears here should be treated with appropriate caution. One day, perhaps, the full truth will emerge.

In the mid-1990s, the Sultan and his brother were assembling a truly fabulous collection of exotic cars. Among them were several that were specially created for them by Bentley Motors.

One order that reached Bentley's Crewe works was for six high-performance luxury 4×4s. As there was no Bentley 4×4 in production at the time, this called for more than the usual amount of lateral thinking, but a decision was made to buy the best 4×4 that was available, and to modify it as appropriate. The choice fell on the latest Range Rover.

The job was supposedly sub-contracted to the Jankel Group, which had had a contract with Rolls-Royce to build long-wheelbase derivatives of the Silver Spur limousine between 1983 and 1989, and under its own name also built a number of bespoke conversions. However, it seems probable that Jankel sub-contracted some of the work. Certainly a Bentley employee of the time remembered visiting a workshop at Southam in Warwickshire to do some work on the vehicles when they were new.

The Range Rovers were modified to accommodate Bentley's long-serving 6.75-litre V8 engine in its turbocharged Continental R form. Standard engines delivered 385bhp, but the engines in these vehicles may well have been the 500bhp twin-turbo 'Sultan-spec' variant that was used in other special Bentley models for Brunei. The Range Rover shells gained new front ends incorporating a Bentley grille, and had other cosmetic features that differentiated them from the parent vehicle. As for cost, there is no real evidence, but it has been rumoured that each one of these very special vehicles cost £3 million.

The best sources suggest that these six vehicles were delivered in 1996, although 1998 has also been suggested. They were certainly known as Bentley Dominator types, and research has uncovered their VINs, the serial numbers of which ran from 422 to 427. There were various different combinations of prefix code which have not yet been interpreted. A sample VIN is SCBTH98C2TCH00426, which is known to have been registered as BQ7570 in Brunei.

CONVERSIONS IN THE USA

During the period of the second-generation Range Rover's production, North American safety and emissions regulations were different enough from those in most other countries to deter specialists from undertaking conversions for US customers. Nevertheless, the USA had a thriving home-grown custom-building industry, largely based in California, which carried out some interesting conversions of the 38A for US clients.

It is not possible to provide information about all of these conversions, many of which were probably completely unique. There are, for example, no known pictures of a six-door limousine on an extended wheelbase that was supposedly built for a hotel in the ski resort of Aspen, Colorado. However, some details are available concerning the convertible built by specialist Richard Straman, and about the Cameron Concepts supercharged models.

The Richard Straman Convertible

Richard Straman was running an established conversions business in Costa Mesa, California, by the time of the 38A Range Rover. The combination of the Californian climate and its population of wealthy celebrities and businesspeople had led to demand for open cars – especially during the period when major manufacturers had stopped building them for fear of US legislation – and Straman had stepped up to the challenge. By the mid-1990s, he was best known for turning closed Ferrari and Mercedes-Benz models into convertibles, and had also worked on some Japanese coupés as well. The company enjoyed a good reputation, and was therefore an obvious choice for an individual who wanted a convertible Range Rover.

It seems probable that only the one example was built, and even the date of that is not certain. However, the fact that it was based on a 4.0 SE and not a top-model 4.6 HSE does tend to suggest that it was commissioned when only the 4.0 SE was available in the USA – so, during 1995. The conversion was considerably more complicated than is apparent from photographs, and supposedly took a year to complete. Among the more difficult elements must have been restoring the strength of the Range Rover's body after the roof had been removed. One way or the other, when Straman announced his company's willingness to build more examples, he quoted a price of $100,000. At that stage, which was probably during 1996, a standard 4.6 HSE cost $62,000 and a 4.0 SE cost $55,000.

The Straman conversion turned the Range Rover into a two-door model, with specially fabricated rear wing panels, and each front door extended by 20cm (nearly 8in) to give good access to the rear seats. A central rollover bar was fitted behind the doors, partly to provide rollover safety but no doubt also to add to the reinforcement of the roofless body. The convertible top was, of course, power-operated, and the interior was given a full Connolly leather treatment, presumably therefore covering moulded plastic items such as the dashboard and centre console as well as the seats and door cards.

Cameron Concepts

Cameron Concepts was based at Newport Beach in California, and was the brainchild of Peter Cameron. The company was already in the business of upgrading American SUVs, and from the mid-1990s it turned its hand to Range Rovers as well. Renamed Special Vehicle Concepts (SVC) early in the new century, the company moved to 1945 Placentia Ave, Unit B, Costa Mesa, CA 92627, and the early Cameron Concepts conversions are now often referred to as SVC types.

The 4.6-litre version of the Range Rover was introduced to the USA at the start of 1996, but its performance was no match for some of the performance-oriented SUVs then available in the USA. Wealthy California clients typically wanted the best that was available, and so Cameron Concepts developed a Range Rover upgrade programme around a supercharger installation to give the necessary extra performance. The supercharged Cameron Concepts Range Rover was introduced in 1997 as the Range Rover SSE (Supercharged SE), and on those examples that were not totally de-badged, the H of the factory-applied HSE tailgate badge was replaced by a matching S. The company ensured that its conversion gained the approval of the California Air Resources Board, so that it could be sold in the notoriously emissions-conscious state of California itself.

The supercharger itself was an Eaton M90S type that was mounted on top of the 4.6-litre V8 engine, raising the overall height of the under-bonnet installation so that Cameron Concepts had to design a special bonnet with a bulge in it to clear the supercharger. The engine's cylinder heads were ported and polished, larger valves (made by Manley) were installed, and a performance camshaft was added. A reprogrammed engine-management system finished the job, and the supercharged Cameron Concepts Range Rover 38A delivered 360bhp at 3,600rpm with 410lb/ft of torque at 2,800rpm. The standard 4.6 HSE of the time had 222bhp at 4,750rpm and 300lb/ft at 2,600rpm, so these were very significant increases. Acceleration from zero to 60mph took 7.37sec, and a special exhaust ensured that the vehicle made the right noises in addition to going quickly.

Wisely, Cameron Concepts also uprated the transmission, brakes and suspension. They modified the shift programme for the standard ZF automatic gearbox, and added limited-slip differentials. There were cross-drilled ventilated discs and stainless-steel braided hydraulic hoses, plus a choice of 18, 19 and 20in wheels, with high-performance or run-flat tyres. The 20in wheels were three-piece alloys with 9.5in rims riding on Toyo 295/45R20 M+S tyres. The front anti-roll bar was uprated, and a new rear one was added, both mounted on urethane bushes, and Bilstein gas dampers were fitted all round.

Paint was, of course, to order, while window tinting, billet grilles, chromed exhaust tips and special lighting were all available. There was a whole range of interior options, including ultra high-performance audio systems, video or DVD equipment, special wood trims, carbon-fibre trim

Cameron Concepts used a supercharger to get more performance from NAS Range Rovers. This one is on a Thor-engined model.

instead of wood, wood-rim steering wheel, premium carpets, a Phillips CARin satnav, hands-free phone, automatic 911 (emergency) call-up, and a K-40 radar detector system with both forward-facing and rearward-facing inputs. The total cost of a Cameron Concepts Range Rover depended on the customer's choice of options, but could easily add $60,000 at a time when the base 4.6-litre vehicle cost $68,625 in the showrooms.

Between 1997 and 2002, the company claimed to have delivered more than 250 custom-built Range Rovers. Many appear to have been sold through the Land Rover dealership network. Under its new name of SVC, Peter Cameron's company then turned its hand to upgrading the third-generation (L322) Range Rover. It closed down in 2007, after the death of Cameron himself in April that year.

BUYING AND OWNING A 38A

Although the second-generation Range Rover was Land Rover's flagship product in the later 1990s, and although it earned plenty of respect from its users, it has built up quite a reputation as a troublesome machine over the years. You need to be aware of that when considering whether to buy one. However, it is also important to understand where that reputation has come from, because the news is certainly not as bad as some doom-mongers like to make out.

For the first year or so of 38A production, build quality was undoubtedly patchy. The problem was that Land Rover was taking on the manufacture of a new kind of vehicle that incorporated a lot of new technology. Although much of that technology was not new to the motoring world at large, it was certainly new to Land Rover, and it took some time for assembly processes to be adapted to cope with it. The company's owners at BMW were sufficiently concerned

In many respects, the later and better equipped models are a better buy – but really, the deciding factor should always be condition. NICK DIMBLEBY

This German publicity picture suggests the air of luxury and serenity that can come
with a well kept 38A Range Rover. The vehicle is an early 4.6 HSE.

to set up the Operation Achilles programme, which was designed to catch all the build problems and rectify them as the vehicles reached Land Rover dealers for servicing. Potential faults were fixed as quickly as possible, often without the owner being aware that anything special had been done to their vehicle.

Build quality had generally improved by the time of the 1996 models, but it was probably not until 1998 that Land Rover attained the levels of quality control that it wanted. Unfortunately, just as on earlier models, embarrassing things could still happen: warning lights would flash to warn of non-existent problems, and the remote locking could lock you out. In the meantime, the few rogue vehicles that reached owners continued to give the model a bad name.

The next set of problems began to arise as the vehicles worked their way down the second-hand market. As these Range Rovers reached their third, fourth, or later owners and their overall value fell, so often did the level of maintenance that they received. As a result, minor faults were often neglected, and these led to more major ones. Within ten years of the model's introduction, it was not uncommon to find sad and unloved examples that had been more or less abandoned because of the potential cost of fixing faults.

It follows from this that the wisest course of action when buying a 38A Range Rover is, first, not to buy one that has been off the road for some time and needs unspecified work, and second, to buy one with a full documented service history as proof that it has been properly maintained. The

**Many second-generation Range Rovers have been customized to suit their owners' tastes.
This one won the class for customized Land Rovers at a magazine-sponsored event.**

complexity of the vehicle's systems is also so great that it is risky to buy an example that has been modified, except perhaps cosmetically. (Obviously the modifications to standard specification available under the Autobiography scheme are an exception to this rule.)

With those warnings in mind, it is important to remember that the second-generation Range Rover can deliver a rewarding ownership experience if it is treated properly. It is a comfortable, refined and capable vehicle with features that still allow it to qualify as luxury transport more than a decade and a half after the last ones were built. The later models in particular have very high levels of equipment and

generally much better build quality than the early ones, and are probably a better bet if you intend to use your vehicle a lot.

THE EXTERIOR

Many Range Rovers have led pampered lives, and it is not uncommon to find an exterior that is nearly blemish free. However, it is a rare example that does not show a few scuff marks on the bumpers at each corner! The paintwork is likely to be generally good unless a vehicle has been mistreated, although it is worth checking for paint bubbling under the wheel arches. This is rarely serious, but should be dealt with at the earliest opportunity.

Unlike their predecessors, these Range Rovers rarely suffer from corrosion in the body – so rarely, in fact, that the presence of corrosion suggests a poorly executed accident repair. There are two areas that repay close inspection, however. One is the bottom edge of the lower tailgate, where water gets in where the outer skin is wrapped over the frame and can set up rusting; open the tailgate to look, and check the inside of the lower edge, below the trim panel. The second potential problem area is the rear of each body sill, but corrosion is not common here and will not normally be found on a Range Rover that has been well looked after.

Some owners have modified their vehicles to look newer than they are, by adding the smoked rear light lenses, clear front indicator lenses, and 'masked' headlamps of the later models. Whether this matters is down to individual preference.

WHEELS

As wheels are now considered an important element in a vehicle's appearance, many owners have altered their Range Rovers cosmetically by fitting new or unusual wheel styles. Buyers who are looking for originality may baulk at this; others will simply accept the vehicle as it is. However, there are

a couple of points that are worth knowing when looking at the wheels on a 38A Range Rover.

First of all, the model was designed around the 16in wheel diameter that was then standard on Land Rover products. The suspension was designed to work at its best with 16in wheels, and it still does. It is also true that the tyres available for 16in wheels generally have strong and flexible sidewalls that are resistant to damage when driving off-road.

To meet public demand, Land Rover did introduce 18in wheels on top models and as an option. The larger wheels certainly do look good on the vehicle – especially the star-spoke Mondial type and the later split-spoke Hurricane type. However, the shallower sidewalls of the tyres associated with these wheels are less flexible than those of the 16in

Wheels can make a big difference to the way a Range Rover looks, and to the way it rides. This is the Triple Sport accessory wheel.

The Stratos wheel later reappeared as the Mirage type, though by then with a 'jewelled' centre cap. NICK DIMBLEBY

Probably the most attractive wheel used on the Range Rover was the 18in Mondial style. NICK DIMBLEBY

tyres, and in some circumstances ride quality can suffer. Those sidewalls are also less resistant to damage while driving off-road, and they do not protect the alloy rims from damage as well as the taller sidewalls of 16in tyres. In town use, there is also a greater risk of kerbing damage to the wheels.

Some owners have fitted aftermarket wheels with diameters larger than 18in. While some of these wheels undoubtedly look good, there is no doubt that the even shallower tyre sidewalls present a greater risk of kerbing damage, make the ride much more knobbly, and are more prone to off-road damage.

THE INTERIOR

The interior of a 38A Range Rover is a very cossetting place to be, especially in the later models with higher levels of equipment. Early models with cloth seats and less wood trim are less obviously luxurious. The leather upholstery is hard-wearing, but look for dry leather and cracks, which will eventually lead to splits. Replacement panels can be sewn in by an expert in the trade.

However, there are two areas of interior trim that do cause problems. One is the A and B pillars, which have a fuzzy flock covering that flakes and breaks off; some owners scrape it off altogether, and others have the pillars

Some owners have added big-diameter aftermarket wheels to their vehicles. This is a 20in design.

retrimmed in leather. The other is the headlining, which comes unglued from its backing pad and droops. The most effective solution is a replacement, and top-quality after-market types can be had from specialists.

Wet footwells indicate leaks, and the usual cause is failure of a pair of rubber O-rings between the heater hoses and the heater matrix. This is becoming quite a common problem as the vehicles get older, and although the O-rings themselves are cheap, fitting them is awkward and time-consuming. It will be expensive in labour costs if entrusted to a specialist.

On the dashboard, check that all digits are correctly displayed on the message centre within the speedometer and on the heater control panel. A book symbol on the heater panel means there is a fault, and a common problem with

The interior trim on early models was quite Spartan by later standards. This is the dashboard of an early SE or DSE model. NICK DIMBLEBY

By later Range Rover standards, a manual gearshift seems out of place, but some owners like them. NICK DIMBLEBY

ABOVE: **An early interior in an SE or a DSE. By later standards it is quite sombre – which was what Land Rover thought the buyers wanted.** NICK DIMBLEBY

Even the load bay of a 30th Anniversary model is beautifully trimmed.

the system is failure of one of the servo motors that control the airflow flaps. These motors can be bought individually as replacements.

Most important when checking over a potential purchase is to make sure that all the dashboard switches do what they are supposed to do, and do not prompt error messages on the message centre panel. Check, too, that other control switches (such as those for the power-adjusted front seats) operate correctly.

ENGINES

The choice of engine is important, because the different engines give a very different character to the 38A. If head rules heart, the BMW diesel is the logical choice because of its reasonable fuel economy (up to 25mpg (11.3ltr/100km) overall). However, the truth is that this engine struggles a little with the weight of the Range Rover, so that acceleration is disappointing even though cruising speeds are comfortable. Some owners have had the engines 'chipped' (with a different electronic engine-management program) to get better performance. However, in some cases, this puts extra strain on the engine and leads to problems such as overheating.

If heart rules head, the 4.6-litre V8 is the only choice. However, although it offers the best acceleration (and the highest top speed, where that is relevant), it also offers the worst fuel consumption. Owners have to live with about 15mpg (18.9ltr/100km) on a regular basis, although it is possible to do better with gentle use – but nobody buys the 4.6-litre Range Rover to use it gently.

As a result, the best bet is probably the 4.0-litre model. It is considerably quicker than the diesel, though not quite as quick as the 4.6. It is also less thirsty than the 4.6 (at around 17mpg (16.6ltr/100km)), but of course nowhere near as economical as the diesel.

All these engines have weaknesses to consider. Overheating is a particular problem with the diesel, and leads to head gasket failure and sometimes to a cracked cylinder head as well. When looking at a diesel model as a potential purchase, allow the engine to idle for a while to see if it starts to run hot – and expect trouble in the longer term if it does.

A problem with the V8s is that the cylinder liners can work loose, and this can be expensive to rectify. The best solution is a full rebuild with 'top hat' liners that are anchored firmly in the block, but this is expensive. Any

This later interior (in a 1998 Vogue 50) is infinitely more attractive – but all that light-coloured leather is just waiting to get dirty. NICK DIMBLEBY

cooling system problems should be investigated carefully, as among the symptoms of loose liners are loss of coolant and overheating. On high-mileage or neglected engines, the hydraulic tappets may fail to take up clearances and cause a very noticeable rattle at the top end of the engine. The usual reason is that the tappets themselves have become blocked with sludge, and that is typically the result of neglected oil changes.

Some owners have attempted to reduce the cost of running a V8 Range Rover by converting it to run on LPG. There are mixed benefits: the fuel certainly is cheaper, but there is usually a slight loss of performance. There are also varying standards of conversion, and it is unwise to buy a converted vehicle that does not come with a fitter's certificate and proof that the LPG system has been serviced according to the manufacturer's recommendations. As for converting a Range Rover that is still running on petrol, the cost of the conversion is likely to be a deterrent, and will only be recouped after many thousands of miles.

TRANSMISSION

Neither the ZF automatic gearbox nor the R380 manual is known for major problems. Although there were quality control problems with early R380s, these were dealt with under warranty at the time. High-mileage automatics may slur between gears, but reconditioned gearboxes are available from specialists.

Check that low range in the transfer box can be selected properly. It is selected by a servo motor, and either this or its linkage may seize through lack of use. Remember that many owners have never used low range in their lives!

On road test, listen for clunks and bangs in the drivetrain when setting off from rest, as these indicate worn components – UJs, differentials, or perhaps suspension bushes. Although it will usually be possible to feel when D or R are selected in an automatic gearbox, there should not be any serious jerks or clunks from underneath. Be especially vigilant if the Range Rover you are testing has a towbar: a lot of heavy towing may have caused wear in the drivetrain, as well as the suspension.

Never forget that the 38A Range Rover is a formidable off-road performer in standard form. This one was being demonstrated at the launch event in Angola in the mid-1990s.

Land Rover was always happy to demonstrate the 38A off-road to representatives of the media. This one is about to reveal its impressive wading abilities.

CHASSIS AND SUSPENSION

Rust in the chassis frame will be exceptional, and should be treated with suspicion. Typically it will result from accident damage that has been poorly repaired, so it is worth looking for other traces of that damage and assessing the result.

The air suspension is not as troublesome as rumour suggests, but some owners have given up on it when faced with repeated problems (often caused by neglect). It has been possible for some time to buy a kit of parts to convert the 38A to steel coil springs, but this definitely gives a harsher ride than the air suspension. As a non-factory modification, it should also be declared to insurers. It is also possible to buy an emergency kit that can be carried on the vehicle to re-inflate the suspension if its springs fail to pump up to working height – but this is a 'get-you-home' solution only.

The air springs are robust items, but should be treated as consumables. They can perish or split, particularly at the base where the rubber bag meets its metal retainer, and regular visual checks are a good idea during ownership. A leaking air spring will not only make the Range Rover sit down on its axles, it will also cause the air compressor to work harder to pump it up to the correct height, and that in turn can cause the compressor to burn out. Air springs are not expensive to replace; compressors are more so, and the job is more time-consuming.

Some useful tests can be carried out using the suspension height control switch on the dashboard. With the engine running, set each different height in succession, and watch for error messages appearing on the information centre screen. It is also worth putting the suspension on its lowest setting, and then raising it to its high position. If the operation takes more than a minute or so, the compressor is probably on the way out.

As for the suspension bushes, these are normally quite long-lived, and worn ones will be obvious from either a visual inspection or from a test drive. Fitting the factory-issue bushes between radius arm and front axle requires a special tool that compresses them to fit into the socket. Aftermarket Polybushes are easier to fit, but using the hardest type can cause some deterioration in the ride quality.

BRAKES

The 38A's braking system has ABS as standard, and as the vehicle is started there should be a quiet whirring sound from under the bonnet as the accumulator builds up fluid pressure to operate the ABS system. Faults with the ABS braking should be flagged up by the dashboard warning light, but unscrupulous owners sometimes remove the bulb, so check that it does illuminate when the ignition is switched on and the system goes through its check phase. ABS accumulators are not particularly expensive, but replacement is best left to a specialist. If the ABS warning light does not go out after the vehicle has exceeded 5mph (8km/h), there is a fault that needs attention. Typically it will be a faulty speed sensor at one of the wheels, or a worn hub.

As for the hardware, brake discs simply bolt on and are therefore easy to change. Hub bearings can be replaced as a DIY job, but it is necessary to have access to a hydraulic press. Many owners simply change the whole hub, which is easier and not prohibitively expensive.

ELECTRICAL EQUIPMENT

The 38A was designed with an array of electrical equipment that was new to Land Rover, and that electrical equipment is one of the model's Achilles heels. Malfunctions can often be caused by something as mundane as a dirty or corroded earth contact, but it often takes a great deal of persistence to find out where that earth contact actually is!

A diagnostic plug is part of the OBD (On Board Diagnostics) system, and allows the BECM (Body Electronic Control Module) memory to be interrogated so that faults can be identified. This could originally be done only through Land Rover's own system, which was called Testbook, but various aftermarket versions have since become available and some are surprisingly affordable. Although these are not all capable of re-setting systems after a malfunction, they will show what the likely cause of a problem is, thus allowing you to decide whether to try to fix it yourself or to take it to a specialist.

The more switches there are, the more there is to go wrong, unfortunately! This switch controls the height settings of the suspension, and should always be checked for correct functioning.
NICK DIMBLEBY

All 38A models were originally supplied with two electronic key fobs, and it is advisable to ensure that both are still with the vehicle. Replacement fobs are expensive, and also have to be programmed individually before they will work correctly with the immobilizer system. Associated with this is that the central-locking receiver unit may become 'confused' by radio signals from a nearby mobile phone transmitter mast. Sometimes the vehicle will then refuse to unlock; sometimes it will unlock with the remote fob, but opening a door will then trigger the anti-theft alarm.

Another well-known problem is that the BECM 'loses' the electronic code for the immobilizer that has to be transmitted to the engine ECU before the vehicle will start. Inevitably, the vehicle will then not start. It is possible to buy an aftermarket re-synchronization device that plugs into the diagnostic socket, and some owners keep this in the glovebox as an insurance against repeat performances; however, these devices are not cheap.

A common cause of this problem is a low battery voltage, which is itself common because of the multiple demands on the battery even when the engine is switched off. Using a trickle charger is therefore a good idea if the vehicle remains unused for long periods. Having the correct battery helps, too: the V8s have a 72Ah type, but the diesels need a 107Ah battery.

CLUBS AND SUPPORT

Finally, it is worth remembering that whatever may go wrong with your 38A Range Rover, it will have happened to somebody else at some time. There are several good specialists who can help you out (although Land Rover's own dealers may not be keen to work on such old models), and there is plenty of advice available on the web. A word of advice about that advice, though: like much of what is on the web, it represents the unfiltered opinions or experience of individuals, and may not be accurate!

There are clubs, too, where you can find support. In the UK, the Range Rover Register caters for Range Rovers of all ages, and many of its members own 38A models. The club can easily be found on the web through a search engine.

Many other off-road and Land Rover clubs welcome 38A owners, but there are certainly some whose attitude towards these models is ambivalent. Do not be put off by such people; if you like the 38A, you will soon find people elsewhere who share your enthusiasm and will enable you to get even more enjoyment from your vehicle.

VIN CODES AND ENGINE NUMBERS

The VIN of a Range Rover 38A will be found in two easily accessible places on the vehicle. It is stamped into a plate mounted on the bonnet shut platform (near the bonnet catch), and also into a plate mounted behind the windscreen at the bottom left as you look forward, where it is visible through the glass.

VIN CODES FOR THE RANGE ROVER 38A

The following VIN codes are for all 38A models except the North American ones. Range Rover 38A VIN codes consist of seventeen characters, made up of an eleven-character prefix code and a six-digit serial number.

Example: SALLPAMJ3MA-123456
(Note: The dash has been added for clarity and is not present on the actual VIN plates.)

This breaks down as follows:

SAL	Manufacturer code (Rover Group)
LP	Range Rover 38A
A	Standard (108in) wheelbase
M	Four-door body
J	4.6-litre V8 petrol engine
	M = 4.0-litre V8 petrol engine
	W = 2.5-litre 6-cylinder diesel engine
3	RHD with automatic gearbox
	4 = LHD, automatic
	7 = RHD with five-speed manual gearbox
	8 = LHD with five-speed manual gearbox
M	Model-year 1995

	T = 1996	Y = 2000	
	V = 1997	I = 2001	
	W = 1998	2 = 2002	
	X = 1999		
A	Assembled at Solihull		
123456	Serial number		

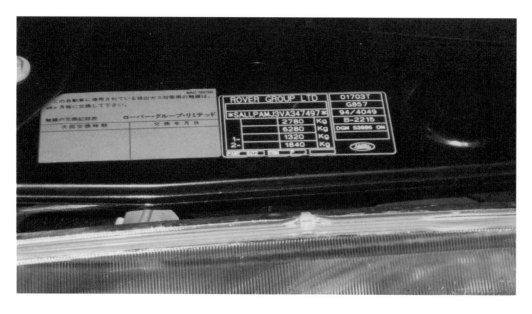

The VIN plate on a 1997 model for Japan, with an additional sticker in Japanese. The manufacturer is Rover Group.

VIN CODES FOR NORTH AMERICAN MODELS

The codes again consist of seventeen characters, made up of an eleven-character prefix code and a six-digit serial number.

Example: SALPA124ISA-123456.
(Note: The dash has been added for clarity and is not present on the actual VIN plates.)
   This breaks down as follows:

SAL	Manufacturer code (Land Rover)
P	Range Rover 38A
A	Class E, with GEMS engine management
	C = Class E, with Callaway engine
	E = Class E, to Californian specification
	F = Class E, 2000MY, to LEV standards
	L = Class E, feature spec 1
	M = Class E, feature spec 2
	V = Class E, with Bosch engine management
I	Four-door body
2	4.0-litre V8 petrol engine
	4 = 4.6-litre V8 petrol engine
	5 = 4.0-litre V8 to LEV standards
	6 = 4.6-litre V8 to LEV or ULEV standards
	9 = 4.6-litre V8
4	LHD with four-speed automatic gearbox
I	Security check digit (0 to 9, or X)
S	Model-year 1995

	T = 1996		W = 1998		Y = 2000
	V = 1997		X = 1999		I = 2001

A	Assembled at Solihull
123456	Serial number

ENGINE NUMBERS

BMW Diesel Engines

The identification number of a BMW turbocharged diesel engine is stamped into the left-hand side of the cylinder block, just above the sump joint.

   These numbers follow the BMW system, which uses a seventeen-digit number. The first ten digits are identifiers, which include a build date code, and the final six digits are a serial number.

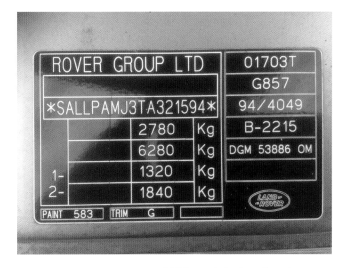

The **VIN** plate on a 1996 model; the plate is always located on the bonnet shut platform. The manufacturer is Rover Group.

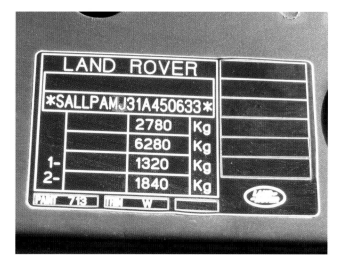

The **VIN** plate on a 2001 model. The manufacturer is Land Rover (after the Ford takeover). The plate also omits the information from the right-hand set of boxes.

Land Rover V8 Engines

The identification number of a V8 petrol engine is stamped into a ledge machined into the side of the cylinder block, next to the dipstick tube. The compression ratio is also stamped into this ledge: normally this is 9.34:1 or 9.38:1, but it may be 8.13:1 on some low-compression engines for export.

The identification number of a V8 engine consists of a three-digit alphanumeric prefix code, followed by a six-digit serial number and a suffix letter. So a typical example might be 46D-123456A (the dash separating the prefix from the serial number has been added for clarity and is not present on the actual engine). The suffix letter indicates minor design changes of importance when servicing the engine. (Note: SAI below refers to Secondary Air Injection.)

42D	4.0-litre, 9.35:1; injection; 1994–1998
44D	4.0-litre, probably 8.13:1; injection; 1994–1998
46D	4.6-litre, 9.35:1; injection; 1994–1998
48D	4.6-litre, probably 8.13:1; injection; 1994–1998
57D	4.0-litre; low-compression; injection; 1998–2001
58D	4.0-litre; high-compression; injection; 1998–2001
59D	4.6-litre; low compression; injection; 1998–2001
60D	4.6-litre; high compression; injection; 1998–2001
61D	4.0-litre; injection; Canada SAI, stripped engine; 1998–2001
62D	4.0-litre; injection; Canada SAI, short engine; 1998–2001
63D	4.6-litre; injection; Canada SAI, stripped engine; 1998–2001
64D	4.6-litre; injection; Canada SAI, short engine; 1998–2001
65D	4.6-litre; injection; NAS SAI, stripped engine; 1998–-2001
66D	4.6-litre; injection; NAS SAI, short engine; 1998–-2001
67D	4.0-litre; injection; NAS SAI, stripped engine; 1998–2001
68D	4.0-litre; injection; NAS SAI, short engine; 1998–2001
73D	4.0-litre; low compression; stripped engine; 1998–2001
74D	4.0-litre; low compression; short engine; 1998–-2001
75D	4.0-litre; high compression; stripped engine; 1998–-2001
76D	4.0-litre; high compression; short engine; 1998–2001
77D	4.0-litre; high compression; Canada; stripped engine; 1998–2001
78D	4.0-litre; high compression; Canada; short engine; 1998–2001
79D	4.6-litre; low compression; stripped engine; 1998–2001
80D	4.6-litre; low compression; short engine; 1998–2001
81D	4.6-litre; high compression; stripped engine; 1998–2001
82D	4.6-litre; high compression; short engine; 1998–2001
83D	4.6-litre; high compression; Canada; stripped engine; 1998–2001
84D	4.6-litre; high compression; Canada; short engine; 1998–2001
92D	4.0-litre; low compression; Canada SAI; 1998–2001
93D	4.6-litre; Canada SAI; 1998–2001
95D	4.0-litre; high compression; NAS SAI; 1998–2001
96D	4.6-litre; NAS SAI; 1998–2001

PAINT CODES

Land Rover used a large number of different paints on the Range Rover 38A over the years. This table provides a key to the codes used for each paint.

	Paint type	Paint code
AA Yellow	Solid	LRC 584, FUN
Alpine White	Solid	LRC 456, NUC
Altai Silver	Metallic	LRC 567, MUM
Alveston Red	Micatallic	LRC 696, CDX
Arles Blue	Solid	LRC 424, JUH
Aspen Silver	Metallic	LRC 458, MUD
Atlantis Blue	Micatallic	LRC 632, JYW
Avalon Blue	Micatallic	LRC 575, JUV
Beluga Black	Solid	LRC 416, PUE
Biarritz Blue	Micatallic	LRC 965, JRJ
Blenheim Silver	Metallic	LRC 642, MAL
Bonatti Grey	Metallic	LRC 659, LAL
Borrego Yellow	Solid	LRC 757, FUQ
British Racing Green	Metallic	LRC 617, HNA
Caledonian Blue	Solid	LRC 507, JUT
Caprice Green	Micatallic	LRC 533, UMQ
Charleston Green	Metallic	LRC 610, HET
Chawton White	Solid	LRC 603, NAL
Cobar Blue	Metallic	LRC 624, JAV
Coniston Green	Solid	LRC 637, HYJ
Epsom Green	Micatallic	LRC 961, HAF
Icelandic Blue	Micatallic	LRC 621, JEL

	Paint type	Paint code
Java Black	Micatallic	LRC 697, PNF
Kent Green	Micatallic	LRC 647, HEX
Montpellier Red	Micatallic	LRC 536, CUY
Monza Red	Solid	LRC 590, CCZ
Niagara Grey	Metallic	LRC 574, LVD
Oslo Blue	Micatallic	LRC 644, JFM
Oxford Blue	Micatallic	LRC 602, JSJ
Portofino Red	Solid	LRC 390, CUF
Rioja Red	Micatallic	LRC 601, CAQ
Riviera Blue	Metallic	LRC 588, JAM
Roman Bronze	Metallic	LRC 479, GUA
Rutland Red	Solid	LRC 607, CPQ
Sahara Gold	Micatallic	LRC 583, GUD
Tintern Green	Micatallic	LRC 656, HEW
Vienna Green	Micatallic	LRC 751, HES
White Gold	Metallic	LRC 618, GMN
Willow Green	Metallic	LRC 970, HOR
Wimbledon Green	Pearlescent	LRC 713, HFM
Woodcote Green	Micatallic	LRC 623, HPE
Zambezi Silver	Metallic	LRC 737, MVC

AUTOBIOGRAPHY PAINT, BADGE AND TRIM OPTIONS

Autobiography customers could ask for any paint colour they liked on their Range Rovers, and most requests could be accommodated. However, the Autobiography team did have a selection of their own colours that suited the vehicle, and would suggest these to a customer who was undecided. All Range Rovers that had a special Autobiography paint finish started life with black paint so that the engine bay remained black after the Autobiography paint had been applied.

In June 2000, the following twenty-two colours made up the 'standard' Autobiography paint palette. At that stage, an Autobiography tailgate badge in solid brass could be had, plated in 18-carat gold or in high quality chrome. The badge was a no-cost option: buyers could choose to have no badge at all, the Autobiography badge with the base model badge, or the Autobiography badge on its own.

Colour	Code	Colour	Code
Auckland Blue	ZXR	Deep Windsor Pearl	ZXS
Aztec	AYS	Gypsy Blue	ZXP

Colour	Code	Colour	Code
Azul	JBT	Iris	KMZ
Black Cherry	PBB	Juniper	JBU
Blaze	CVA	Miami	JBX
British Racing Green	HNA	Monsoon	ZXG
Cayman	EAF	Prairie Rose	ZXQ
Crimson	CBB	Savannah	JBW
Crystal	MUT	Seguarro	HFK
Damson	ZZZ	Volcano	EAC
Daytona	FAP	Wimbledon	HFM

When upholstered under the Autobiography scheme, seats had high quality Cheshire-grade leather, and could be had in three styles. The Classic style could be had with either three-flute or six-flute wearing surfaces, and when ordered with contrasting colours, the seat facing colour also flowed over the headrests and backrest. The Contemporary style had a three-flute facing with plain upper backrest panels. The Traditional style had six-flute seat facings, with the optional contrast colour only on the facings.

In June 2000, there were twenty-five 'recommended' Autobiography leather colours. These included the standard production colours. Customers could, of course, also specify their own colours, but over 30,000 different combinations could be made from the recommended colours and the three different styles of leather. The colours were:

Colour	Code	Colour	Code
Amazon	85076	Magnolia	40867
Ash Grey	40863	Monaco	85074
Beechnut	40874	Moroccan Sand	85157
Burgundy	40864	Parchment	40870
Caspian	85079	Prussian Blue	85156
Ceylon	85080	Rowan Berry Red	85155
Classic Green	85138	Saddle	40855
Dark Granite	40858	Slate Blue	40865
Fuchsia	85075	Solar Flare	85077
Ivory	85154	Sunset	85073
Lichen	40871	Walnut	85045
Light Granite	40857	Wild Sage	40875
Lightstone Beige	40852		

PRODUCTION FIGURES

SERIAL NUMBERS

The numbers shown below are the first and last serial numbers for each calendar year (NOT for each model-year). Note that vehicles did not always come down the lines in strict serial-number order!

1993	300001 to 300009	(pre-production vehicles)
1994	300010 to 305886	
1995	305887 to 331317	
1996	331318 to 360754	
1997	360755 to 390817	
1998	390818 to 417379	
1999	417380 to 435581	
2000	435582 to 453834	
2001	453835 to 467128	(last vehicle on 13 December 2001)

ANNUAL BUILD TOTALS

These figures are again for the calendar year.

1993	9
1994	5,887
1995	25,431
1996	29,437
1997	30,063
1998	26,562
1999	18,202
2000	18,253
2001	13,293

These figures give a total of 167,137 examples. Land Rover usually omits the nine pre-production examples built in 1993, and quotes the figure of 167,128.

UK PRICES 1994–2002

These figures are showroom prices for Range Rover models without extras. All figures are inclusive of Value Added Tax (VAT). From October 1996, Land Rover quoted an 'on the road' (OTR) price that included VAT, number plates, twelve months' road tax and a first service charge.

Date	Model	Price (£)	Remarks
1995 June	4.0	32,850	
	2.5 DT	32,850	
	4.0 SE	37,200	
	2.5 DSE	37,200	Manual gearbox only
	4.6 HSE	44,850	
1995 Oct	2.5 DSE Auto	38,650	
1996 Oct	Autobiography	61,190.43	Example price only
1997 July	HSE+	53,000	
	CARiN edition	63,000	
1998 June	dHSE	47,075	
	Vogue 50	68,000	
	Vogue 50 CARiN	71,000	
1998 Sep	2.5 DT	39,640	
	4.0	40,995	Automatic only
	2.5 DSE	42,700	
	4.0 SE	44,055	
	4.6 HSE	51,165	

Date	Model	Price (£)	Remarks
1998 Dec	County SE	42,595	Diesel or 4.0
	Vogue SE	54,495	4.6
1999 Mar	2.5 DT	39,645	
	4.0	41,000	Automatic only
	2.5 DSE	42,705	
	4.0 SE	44,060	Automatic only
	2.5 DHSE	48,705	
	4.6 HSE	51,170	
1999 Sep	County	40,000	Diesel or 4.0
	2.5 DSE manual	42,000	Special order only
	2.5 DHSE	46,000	
	4.0 HSE	46,000	
	4.6 Vogue	53,000	
	Holland & Holland	65,000	Estimated price
	Linley	100,000	
2000 July	County	40,000	Formerly £41,375
	4.6 Vogue	53,000	Formerly £53,995
2000 Oct	County	40,000	Diesel or 4.0
	HSE	46,000	Diesel or 4.0
	Vogue	53,000	4.6 only
	30th Anniversary	57,500	Plus £6,000 for DVD
	Holland & Holland	64,495	Plus £5,000 for TV & video
	Linley	100,000	
2001 Feb	County	36,995	Diesel or 4.0
	HSE	42,995	Diesel or 4.0
	Vogue	49,995	4.6 only
2001 Sep	Bordeaux	38,995	Diesel or 4.0
	Westminster	46,495	Diesel or 4.0
	Vogue SE	53,995	4.6 only; plus £4,000 for DVD

INDEX

RELATED TITLES FROM CROWOOD

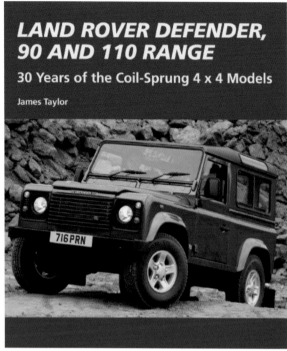

Land Rover Defender 90 and 110 Range
ISBN 978 1 84797 453 2

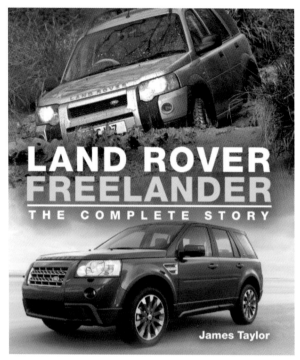

Land Rover Freelander
ISBN 978 1 78500 326 4

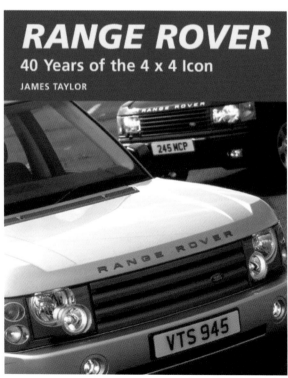

Range Rover: 40 Years of the 4 x 4 Icon
ISBN 978 1 84797 184 5

Range Rover First Generation
ISBN 978 1 78500 411 7